HORIZON READERS

BEAVERS

PAGES FROM THE WRITINGS OF
GREY OWL

Edited by

E. E. REYNOLDS

ILLUSTRATED BY STUART TRESILIAN

T0351986

CAMBRIDGE
AT THE UNIVERSITY PRESS
1940

CAMBRIDGE UNIVERSITY PRESS
Cambridge, New York, Melbourne, Madrid, Cape Town,
Singapore, São Paulo, Delhi, Tokyo, Mexico City

Cambridge University Press
The Edinburgh Building, Cambridge CB2 8RU, UK

Published in the United States of America by
Cambridge University Press, New York

www.cambridge.org
Information on this title: www.cambridge.org/9781107600287

First published 1940
First paperback edition 2011

A catalogue record for this publication is available from the British Library

ISBN 978-1-107-60028-7 Paperback

Cambridge University Press has no responsibility for the persistence or
accuracy of URLs for external or third-party internet websites referred to in
this publication, and does not guarantee that any content on such websites is,
or will remain, accurate or appropriate.

Grey Owl

Who was Grey Owl?

PEOPLE still argue as to whether Grey Owl was really an Indian by birth or only by adoption. What is certain is that about 1905 he began work as a canoeman and voyageur on the rivers and in the vast forests of Canada. For a time he lived with a band of Ojibway Indians on an island in Lake Temagami. He quickly learned their language and became so much one of them that they adopted him. They gave him the name of Wa-Sha-Quon-Asin, which means, 'He who walks by night', for they noticed how fond he was of travelling after sunset. That Ojibway name has been translated into English as GREY OWL.

He soon became known as an expert woodsman and trapper; he showed a reckless courage in face of the many dangers and emergencies that meet the traveller in that wild country; he came to know the ways of rivers, of rapids, and of the animals of the forests.

Then came the outbreak of war in 1914. He enlisted under the name of Archie Belaney, and for three years fought in France as a sniper. He was wounded and gassed, and at the end of 1917 was discharged and sent back to Canada. The lameness from his wound, and his weakened health made it impossible for him to follow his old strenuous life, so he turned to trapping.

It was not long before a change came over him. Perhaps as a result of all the suffering he had seen in France, he began to feel sorry for the animals he trapped, and at length he decided to give up an occupation which meant so much cruelty. For a time he suffered greatly; his small army pension was not enough to live on, so he began to write down accounts of his experiences.

He recalled the old times on the rivers as a canoeman, and the risks and dangers of the trail. Then he set down what he knew of the Indians and their way of living, and next he wrote of some new friends he had made—the Beavers. He had found his mission. He would try to make people kinder to animals; he would do all he could to preserve the great forests of

Canada, and lastly he would try to save the remnants of the race that had adopted him.

He wrote four books: *The Men of the Last Frontier*, which tells of the old days as a voyageur; *Tales of an Empty Cabin*, in which he records many of his adventures in the woods; *Pilgrims of the Wild*, which is an autobiography containing an account of how he came to protect the beavers; and, *The Adventures of Sajo and her Beaver People*, a story of two young Indians and two beavers.

These books made him famous throughout the world. The Canadian Government employed him to guard the wild life round Lake Ajawaan in the Prince Albert National Park, and there he had that wonderful log-cabin which he shared with Jelly Roll, Rawhide, and their family.

He came to England to lecture about his animal friends, and then went on to the United States to speak his message there; his last lecture was given in his own country early in 1938. Then he returned to his cabin and the lake with its forest—and the beavers who were then still sleeping their winter sleep.

Worn out with his long months of constant travel and lecturing, he had no strength to resist illness, and after a short time in hospital, he died on the 13th of April, 1938. They buried him by the shores of his lake where the animals had learned to know him as their friend.

CONTENTS

SAJO AND SHAPIAN

CHAPTER ONE

Big Small and Little Small

The Indian, Gitchie Meegwon, Big Feather, lived with his motherless boy and girl, Shapian and Sajo, in a log-cabin by the shores of a lake in the wild lands of Northern Canada. The place was called O-pee-pee-soway, which means, The Place of Talking Waters.

One day he went out hunting, and found two baby, or kitten-beavers, who had been swept downstream far from their home. Big Feather knew that they would soon die as they were so helpless. So he decided to try to save them. He made a basket of birch bark, and in the bottom he put some bedding of grass, and some green food-stuffs such as beavers love. The kittens soon settled down after a good feed.

Then Big Feather put the basket in his canoe and set off back to his log-cabin; he knew that his little girl, Sajo, would be happy at getting such pets, and the boy, Shapian, who was three years older, would also enjoy looking after the kitten-beavers.

THE kittens quickly took a liking to their new way of living, and although no human beings could ever quite take the place of their own parents, everything possible was done to make them feel at ease.

Shapian partitioned off the under part of his bunk with sheets of birch bark, leaving one end open; and this was their house, in which they at once made themselves very much at home. Gitchie Meegwon cut a hole in the floor and fitted down into it a wash-tub, for a pond, and they spent nearly half their time in it, and would lie on top of the water eating their twigs and leaves. Whenever they left the tub, they always squatted their plump little persons upright beside it, and scrubbed their coats, first squeezing the hair in bunches with their little fists to get the water out. That done, the whole coat was carefully combed with a double claw that all beavers are provided with, one on each hind foot, for this purpose. All this took quite a while, and they were so business-like and serious about it that Sajo would become as interested as they were, and would sometimes help them, rubbing their fur this way and that with the tips of her fingers, and then they would scrub away so much the harder.

They often sat up in this manner while eating the bark off small sticks, and as one or other of them held a stick crossways in his hands, rolling it round and round whilst the busy teeth whittled off the bark, he looked for all the world like some little old man playing on a flute. Sometimes they varied the show, and when the sticks were very slim they ate the whole business, putting one end in their mouths and pushing it in with their hands, while the sharp front teeth, working very fast, chopped it into tiny pieces. The rattle of their cutting machinery sounded much the same as would a couple of sewing-machines running a little wild, and as they held up their heads and shoved the sticks, to all appearances, slowly down their throats, they looked a good deal like a pair of sword-swallowers.

They had to have milk for the first two weeks or so, and Sajo borrowed a baby's bottle from a neighbour in the village, and fed them with it turn about. But while one would be getting his meal (both hands squeezed tight around the neck of the bottle!), the other would scramble around and make a loud outcry and a hubbub, and try to get hold of the bottle, and there would be a squabbling and a great confusion, and the can of milk was sometimes upset and spilled all over; so that at last there had to be another bottle, and Shapian fed one while Sajo fed the other. Later on they were fed with bannock and milk, which made things a little easier, as each had his own small dish which the children held for him. The beavers would pick up the mixture with one hand, shoving it into their mouths at a great rate; and I am afraid their table manners were not very nice, as there was a good deal of rather loud smacking of lips and hard breathing to be heard, and they often talked with their mouths full. But they had one excellent point; they liked to put away their dishes when they had finished, pushing them along the floor into a corner or under the stove; of course if there was a certain amount of milk-soaked bannock left in them, that was quite all right, so far as the beavers were concerned, and by the time the dishes had arrived at their destinations these remains had been well squashed

and trampled on the line of march, and the floor would
be nicely marked up with small, sticky beavers' tracks,
having sometimes to be partly scrubbed.

The larger one of the two was called Chilawee, or
Big Small, and the not-so-large one was called Chikanee, or Little Small. Unfortunately they did not grow
evenly; that is, one would grow a little faster than the
other for a while, and then he would slack down and
the other would catch up, and get ahead of him. First
one was bigger than the other, then the other was
bigger than the one! And it would be discovered that
Little Small had been Big Small for quite some time,
whilst Big Small had been going around disguised as
Little Small.

It was all very confusing, and Sajo had just about
decided to give them one name between them and call
them just 'The Smalls', when Chilawee settled matters
after a manner all his own. He had a habit of falling
asleep in the warm cave under the stove, between the
stones, and one day there was a great smell of burning
hair, and no one could imagine where it came from.
The stove was opened and examined, and swept off,
and the stove-pipes were tapped, and rapped, but the
smell of burning hair was getting stronger all the time;
until someone thought of looking *under* the stove, to
discover Chilawee sleeping there unconcernedly while
the hair on his back scorched to a crisp, and he was
routed out of there with a large patch of his coat badly
singed. This made a very good brand, something like

those that cattle are marked with on a ranch, and it stayed there all Summer, making it very easy to tell who was who; and by calling one of them (the burnt one) *Chila*wee, and the other Chika*nee*, so as to be a little different, they got to know each their name, and everything was straightened out at last.

They were a great pair of little talkers, Chilawee and Chikanee, and were always jabbering together, and sometimes made the strangest sounds. And whenever either of the children spoke to them, which was often, they nearly always answered in a chorus of little bleats and squeals. When there was any work going on, such as the carrying in of water, or wood, or the floor was being swept, or if the people laughed and talked more than usual, or there were any visitors, the two of them would come bouncing out to see what it was all about and try to join in, and they would cut all kinds of capers, and get pretty generally in the way. It had been found that if given any titbits from the table, they always took them into their house to eat or store them. So when they, like bad children, got to be something of a nuisance to the visitors, they had to be bribed with bits of bannock to make them go back in again; but before long, out they would come for some more bannock, and take that in with them, and out again, and so on. And very soon they got to know that visiting time was bannock time as well, and when meal-times came around they knew all about that too, and would be right there, pulling and tugging at the people's clothes and crying out for bannock, and trying to climb up people's legs to get it. And of course they always got what they wanted, and would run off with it to their cabin under the bunk, shaking their heads and hopping along in great style.

They followed the children around continuously, trotting patiently along behind them; and their legs were so very short and they ran so low to the floor on them, that their feet could hardly be seen, so that they looked like two little clockwork animals out of a toy-shop, that went on wheels and had been wound up and never *would* stop. Anything they found on the floor, such as moccasins, kindling wood and so forth, they dragged from place to place, and later, when they got bigger and stronger, they even stole sticks of firewood from the wood-box and took them away to their private chamber, where they sliced them up into shavings with their keen-edged teeth and made their beds with them; and nice, clean-looking beds they were too. Any small articles of clothing that might happen to fall to the floor, if not picked up at once, quickly disappeared into the beaver house. The broom would be pulled down and hauled around, and this broom and the firewood seemed to be their favourite playthings; chiefly, I suspect, on account of the noise they could make with them, which they seemed very much to enjoy.

But their greatest amusement was wrestling. Standing up on their hind legs, they would put their short arms around each other as far as they would go, and with their heads on each other's shoulders, they would try to put each other down. Now, this was hard to do, as the wide tails and the big, webbed hind feet made a very solid support, and they would strain, and push, and grunt, and blow until one of them, feeling himself slipping, would begin to go backwards in order to keep his balance, with the other coming along pushing all he could. Sometimes the loser would recover sufficiently to begin pushing the other way, and then the walk would commence to go in the opposite direction; and so, back and forth, round and round, for minutes at a time, they would carry on this strange game of theirs, which looked as much like two people waltzing as it did anything else. All the while it was going on there would be, between the grunts and gasps, loud squeals and cries from whoever was getting pushed, and much stamping of feet and flopping of tails, trying to hold their owners up, until one of them, on the backward march, would allow his tail to double under him, and fall on his back, when they would immediately quit and scamper around like two madcaps.

But they were not always so lively. There came times when they were very quiet, when they would sit solemnly down together with their hands held tight to their chests and their tails before them, watching whatever was going on, still as two mice, looking, listening without a word, as though they were trying to make out what everything was all about. And sometimes, as they squatted there one beside the other, like two chocolate-coloured kewpies or little manikins, Sajo would kneel in front of them and tell them a story, marking time to the words with her finger before their noses, as though she were conducting an orchestra. And they would sit there and listen, and watch her finger very closely, and soon they would commence to shake their heads up and down and from side to side, as beavers always do when they are pleased, and at last they would shake their whole bodies and their heads so hard that they would topple over and roll on the floor, exactly as if they had understood every word and just couldn't help laughing themselves to pieces over the story. And Shapian would stand by taking it all in, and finding it rather ridiculous; but at the same time he wished —very privately of course—that he was not quite such a man, so he could join in this story-telling business himself.

Sometimes the little fellows were lonely, and would whimper together with small voices in their dark little chamber, and Sajo, who had never forgotten her own mother and knew why they were lonesome, would take them in her arms and croon softly to them, and try to comfort them. And they would snuggle up close to her, holding tight to each other's fur all the while as though afraid to lose one another, and would bury their wee noses in the warm, soft spot in her neck where they so loved to be; and after a while the whimpering would cease and they would perhaps forget, for this time, and

'*Exactly as if they had understood every word and just couldn't help laughing themselves to pieces over the story.*'

they would give big, long sighs and little moans of happiness, and fall asleep.

And especially Chikanee loved Sajo. Chikanee was not as strong as Chilawee, was quieter and more gentle. Chilawee had a rather jolly way about him, and was more of a roisterer, one of those 'all for fun and fun for all' kind of lads to whom life is just one big joke; but Chikanee often had lonesome spells by himself, in corners, and had to be picked up, and petted, and made much of. Often he came out in the night and cried beside Sajo's bed to be taken up and allowed to sleep there beside her—while Chilawee lay on his back in the hut, snoring away like a good fellow. When Chikanee was in some small trouble, such as bumping his nose on the stove, or getting the worst of a wrestling match, he came to Sajo for comfort. And Sajo, always ready to sympathise with him because he was the weaker of the two, would kneel down beside him on the floor; and then Chikanee would climb on to her lap and lie there, happy and contented. Chilawee, when his badness was all done for the day, and he was feeling perhaps a little left out of things, would come over to get *his* share of the petting, squeezing in tight beside Chikanee, where he would settle down after giving a few deep sighs, vastly pleased, no doubt, with his day's work. And Sajo, not wishing to disturb them, would stay there until they were ready to go.

It was very easy to tell them apart by now, as they had become quite different in their ways. Chilawee was stronger, bolder and more adventurous than his chum, a kind of a comical fellow who seemed to enjoy bumping his head on the table-legs, or dropping things on his toes, or falling into the wood-box. He was as inquisitive as a parrot and wanted to be into every-thing, which he generally was, if he could reach it. Once he climbed up on to the edge of a pail of water that someone had left on the floor for a moment, and perhaps mistaking it for a plunge-hole, dived right into it. The pail, of course, upset with a bang, splashing the water in all directions. He was most surprised; and so was everybody else. But in spite of all this wilful behaviour, he was just as affectionate as Chikanee, and dogged Shapian's footsteps (when not otherwise en-gaged!) nearly as much as the other one did Sajo's. And he could not bear to be away from Chikanee very long. Everywhere they went they were together, trotting along one behind the other, or side by side, and if they should become parted on their wanderings in the camp, they would start out to look for each other, and call to one another. And when they met they would sit quite still for a little time, with their heads together, holding each other by the fur—though this wistful mood soon passed off, and it was not long before it all ended up in one of those queer wrestling matches, which seemed to be their way of celebrating.

* * * * * *

And then there came a time when Big Feather said that the kittens should be allowed their freedom. They were now quite a good size, and very active and strong, and the children were a little afraid that they would wander off and be for ever lost. But their father told them how little beavers will not leave their home, if kindly treated, but would always return to the cabin as if it were a beaver house. He said they got lonely very quickly and would only stay away an hour or two.

So, one great, glorious and very exciting day, the barricade that had been kept across the bottom of the doorway was taken away, and out they went. Not all at once, though, for they did a lot of peeping and spying around corners, and sniffed and listened to a whole host of smells and sounds that were not really there at all, and they made two or three attempts before they finally ventured down to the lake, with Sajo and Shapian on either side for a bodyguard. They started off at a very slow and careful walk, sitting up every so often to look around for wolves and bears; of course there weren't any, but it was lots of fun pretending, and as they came closer to the lake the walk became faster, and broke into a trot, which soon became a gallop and into the water they rushed—and then dashed out again, hardly knowing what to make of so large a wash-tub as this. However, they soon went in again, and before very long were swimming, and diving, and screeching, and splashing their tails and having a glorious time, 'Just like real beavers', said Sajo.

It wasn't long before they commenced to chew down

small poplar saplings. These they cut into short lengths, and peeled the bark off them in great enjoyment, while they sat amongst the tall grass and the rushes at the water's edge. They played and wrestled, and ran up and down the shore, and romped with their young human friends, and tore in and out of the water in a great state of mind. They stuck their inquisitive noses into every opening they saw, and found in the bank an empty musk-rat hole. They being just about the same size as the late owner of the hole, this suited them exactly, and they started to dig there. The opening was under water, and as they worked away there the mud began to come out in thick clouds, so that nothing in the water could be seen.

They spent hours at a time digging out the burrow they had found, and when it was far enough back to be safe, as they considered, it was turned upwards and made to come out on top of the ground, and so become a plunge-hole, and over it, to the intense delight of Sajo and Shapian, they built a funny little beavers' house! So now they had a real lodge, with a small chamber in it and an under-water entrance, a tunnel and a plunge-hole, all complete. The lodge was a little shaky about the walls, and was not very well plastered, but it was really quite a serviceable piece of work, considering.

Then they collected a quantity of saplings, and poplar and willow shoots, and made a tiny feed-raft with them in front of their water-doorway, the same as grown-up beavers do, although it was ever so much smaller. They had a warm bed of their own up in the cabin, same as the big folk had, and there was always plenty of bannock, and, on certain occasions, even a taste or two of preserves, and each had his own little dish to eat it out of, so that, counting everything, they owned a considerable amount of property for the size of them and were really quite well-to-do. So they didn't need either the crazy-looking lodge or the feed-raft, but it was great fun fixing things up, 'n'everything—and cutting little trees, and digging, and playing with mud, and doing all those things that beavers like so much to do, and cannot live contentedly without.

Shapian built a play-house by the water-side, and they were often all in there together, while they rested in the shade of it; and this was Chikanee's favourite spot, and he often went there to look for Sajo, and would always come there when she called him. But Chilawee, the adventurer, who was more of a rover, and something of a pirate, I'm inclined to think, could not stay still anywhere very long and would soon ramble away, and was continually getting lost. Of course *he* knew he wasn't lost, but the others thought he was, which amounted to the same thing so far as they were concerned; and then, of course, there would be a hunt. And he would turn up in the most unexpected places, and would be found in the play-house when it was supposed to be empty, or in the cabin when he was supposed to be in the play-house, or hidden away in the beaver wigwam, or under the canoe, where he would be asleep as likely as not. And when found, he would sit upright with his tail out in front of him, and would teeter-totter and wiggle his body and shake his head, as if he were either dancing or laughing at the trick he had played on the rest of them.

Nor was Chikanee quite the saint you may begin to think he was; he had as much fun as any of them. But there were times when he would break off quite suddenly, as though some thought had come into his little head, perhaps some dim memory of his home-pond that was so far away among the Hills. And then, if Sajo were not there to comfort him, he would waddle on his squat little legs, up to the play-house to look for her. If he found her there, he would sit beside her and do his careful toilet; and after he was all tidied up, he would nestle close to this so well-loved companion, and with his head on her knee, try to talk to her in his queer beaver language and tell her what the trouble was; or else lie there with his eyes half-closed and dreamy, making small sounds of happiness, or perhaps of lonesomeness, or love—we cannot know. Very, very good friends indeed were these two, and where one was, there would be the other, before very long.

And what with all the lively antics, and the skylarking, and the work (not too much of it, of course), and all the play, it would be hard for me to tell you just who were the happiest among these youngsters of the Wild, those with four legs, or those with two. But this I *do* know, that they were a very merry crew, in those happy, happy days at O-pee-pee-soway, The Place of Talking Waters.

* * * * * *

The titbits of bannock had been getting smaller and smaller lately. Big Feather had been away some days now to get more provisions, and had not yet returned, and now there was hardly any flour. Nobody, children or beavers, had very much to eat, until one day the four playfellows arrived back at the cabin to find Gitchie Meegwon there.

He looked very grave and troubled about something. But the provisions were there; a bag of flour and some other goods lay on the floor, and beside them stood a white man, a stranger. This man had with him a large box. Big Feather spoke kindly to his children, but he never smiled as he generally did, and they wondered why. The white man, too, stood there without speaking. Somehow things didn't look right. Even the little beavers seemed to feel that there was something amiss, for animals are often quick to feel such things, and they, too, stood there quietly, watching.

And Shapian, who had been to Mission School and understood English fairly well, heard his father say to the man:

'There they are; which one are you going to take?'

What was that! What could he mean? With a sudden sick feeling Shapian looked at his sister; but of course she had not understood.

'Wait till I have a look at them,' said the stranger, answering Big Feather's question. 'Let them move around a bit.' He was a stout, red-faced man with hard blue eyes—like glass, or ice, thought Shapian. But Big Feather's eyes were sad, as he looked at his boy and girl. He asked the white man to wait a moment, while he spoke to his children.

'Sajo, Shapian; my daughter, my son,' he said in Indian, 'I have something to tell you.'

Sajo knew then that some trouble had come to them. She came close to Shapian, and looked timidly at the stranger—why, oh why, was he looking so hard at the beavers?

'Children,' continued their father, 'this is the new trader, from the fur-post at Rabbit Portage; the old one, our good friend, has gone. A new Company has taken over the post, and they ask me to pay my debt. It is a big debt, and cannot be paid until we make our hunt, next Winter. We now have no provisions, as you know, and this Company will give me nothing until the debt is paid. So I must go on a long journey for them, with the other men of the village, moving supplies to the new post at Meadow Lake, which is far from here. My work will pay the debt, and more, but I will receive no money until I return. In the meantime, you, my children, must live. I cannot see you go hungry. This trader will give us these provisions.' Here he pointed at the bags and parcels laying on the floor. 'And in exchange he wants—he wants one of the beavers.' He stopped, and no one so much as moved, not even the beavers, and he continued, 'Live beavers are very valuable, and whichever one he takes will not be killed. But my heart is heavy for you, my children, and—' he looked at Chilawee and Chikanee, 'and for the little beaver that must go.'

Shapian stood very still and straight, his black eyes looking hard at the trader, while Sajo, hardly believing, whispered, 'It isn't true; oh, it isn't true!'

But Shapian never spoke, only put his arm around his sister's shoulder, and stared hard at this man, this stranger who had come to spoil their happiness. He thought of his loaded gun, so close behind him in the corner; but his father must be obeyed, and he never moved. And he looked so fiercely at the trader that, although he was only a fourteen-year-old boy, the man began to feel a little uneasy; so he opened his box, and reaching out for one of the beavers, picked the little fellow up, put him in it and shut down the lid. He nodded to Gitchie Meegwon:

'Well, I'll be seeing you down at the post in a couple of days,' he said, and walked out with the box under his arm, shutting the door behind him.

Just like that.

And then Sajo, without a sound, fell to her knees beside her brother and buried her face in his sleeve.

The trader had chosen Chikanee.

And Chilawee, not knowing what to think, suddenly afraid, went into his little cabin, alone.

CHAPTER TWO

Through Fire and Water

Big Feather went off next day on his journey, and Sajo, Shapian and Chilawee were left alone. They were very unhappy, and little Chilawee spent hours searching for his companion, until Sajo thought her heart would break. She and her brother tried hard to be brave about the loss of Chikanee, but as the days went by, they missed him more and more.

Then one drowsy afternoon, Sajo took Chikawee with her up to the waterfall, and there she went to sleep with him in her lap, and she had a dream. It seemed as if the Waterfall said to her:

> *Sajo, Sajo,*
> *You must go.*
> *To the city,*
> *You must go.*

When she awoke, she hurried back to the cabin and told Shapian of her dream, and said that they must go off to the Big City and fetch back Chikanee. Her brother shook his head: the City was a long way off; they had never been so far away from their lake, and they had no money. But Sajo would not hear of any difficulties: they must go—the Waterfall had told her. So at last Shapian agreed.

LATE the same night everything was in readiness for the journey. It would take them nearly a week to get to the trading post at Rabbit Portage, the first step of their long journey to the city; and they had no idea what lay beyond the post. So they took plenty of everything that was needed for a long trip. Sajo had made several large bannocks, and filled different-sized canvas bags with flour, tea and salt, and she made up a parcel of dried deer meat and set aside a small pail of lard, and put matches in a tight-topped can where they would remain dry; while Shapian rolled up a tent and blankets, fixed up a fish-line, sharpened belt-axe and his hunting-knife, whittled a thin edge on the blades of the paddles, and boxed up whatever pots and dishes and other small items of cookery they would have need of.

The sun had not yet arisen on the following morning when breakfast was over and the full outfit was loaded in the canoe, along with Shapian's rifle; for much as he prized this gun, he intended to sell it if he could, hoping that it would bring at least enough to pay their way to the city. What was to happen after that he didn't dare even to think about. Chilawee went in the same birch-bark basket in which he and Chikanee had first come to O-pee-pee-soway, and in the cookery-box Sajo had put *both* the little beaver dishes, as this helped her to feel more certain that they were going to bring back Chikanee and Chilawee together.

'We will need them both,' she said aloud, 'for'— and here her voice dropped a little—'we *are* going to get him, I think', and then louder, as she nodded her head and pursed her lips, 'I just *know* we are.'

The village was some distance away from their cabin, and they had told no one about their plans, for fear the older people might try to stop them. The old Chief, especially, might forbid them. So they slipped away into the mists of early morning without anyone being the wiser. And as they floated out from the landing, Sajo shook her paddle above her head, as she had seen the men do when they started on a journey, shouting the name of the place they were bound for; and so she held her paddle up and cried out 'Chik-a-*nee*! Chik-a-*nee*!' You could hardly call Chikanee a place, but, she thought, wherever he is, that's where we are going. But Shapian did not wave his paddle, nor did he shout; for he was not so sure about where they would end up.

And so they left the Place of Talking Waters, and started out on what was to be, for all three of them, their Great Adventure.

They stopped occasionally in order to put Chilawee over the side to have a drink and swim around for a minute or two so as to get cool, for the weather was very hot; and that evening they put up their tent in the woods along the shore, and spent the night there. The next morning at daybreak they were away again, and paddled steadily till dark, stopping only to eat and to exercise their furry chum. Each morning they were on their way before the sun rose, and every evening they made camp in some sheltered spot beside the water, where Chilawee swam around all night, always returning to the tent at daylight to fall asleep in his basket,

'*Put Chilawee over the side to have a drink and swim around for a minute or two.*'

where he remained quietly all day. Both children worked on the portages, of which there were a number, each carrying a share of the load. There were two trips apiece, including the canoe, which Shapian carried alone.

And so day after day they forged ahead, onward, onward, ever onward; and two small backs bent and swayed like clockwork, and two paddles swished and dipped all the long day, as regularly and evenly as the step of marching soldiers, while the burning sun rose on one side of them, passed overhead, and sank again like a great red ball behind the dark wall of the forest. Day after day the faithful bark canoe carried them staunchly and steadily forward, outward bound on the long search for the absent Chikanee.

One morning they awoke to find a faint smell of wood-smoke in the air, a smell of burning moss and scorching brush and leaves, and they knew that somewhere, seemingly far away, there was a forest fire. But it was closer than they had at first supposed, for as soon as they were well out on the lake and were able to look about them, they could see an immense pillar of smoke billowing up from behind the distant hills; and they did not paddle very far before they found that their route would bring them more and more in its direction. The lake was getting very narrow, and farther on it ended and became a river, across which the fire could easily jump, and Shapian determined to get through this narrow place as quickly as possible, to a large lake that lay beyond, where they would be safe. So they hurried on, and as they went the smoke spread higher and wider, so that it was no longer a pillar, but a white wall that seemed to reach the sky, and rolled outwards and down in all directions, becoming thicker and thicker until the sun was hidden, and the air became heavy and stifling, and very still. The whole country to the eastward seemed to be on fire, and although the blaze itself was hidden by the hills, even at that distance there could be heard a low moaning sound that never ceased and was, minute by minute, becoming closer, and heading straight towards them—they were right in the path of the fire. The big lake was some distance away, across a portage, and there was no time to be lost if they were to cross over to it before the fire rushed down upon them; for, while some forest fires move slowly, others have been known to travel as fast as thirty miles an hour.

As the hot smoke cooled off, it began to come down, settling in a dark, blue haze over all the land, making far-off points invisible and near ones look dim, so that soon nothing could be seen but the row of trees nearest the shore-line, and the children were only able to keep their right direction by watching this, and by the sound of the rapids that lay ahead of them. Very soon they arrived at the head of this steep place in the river, where the water rushed and foamed wildly between, and over, dark jagged rocks for several hundred yards. It was a dangerous place, but Shapian dared not take time, with the double trip they had, to cross the portage that went round it, and he decided to take the quicker route and run the rapids. For the fire was now not far away, and the sharp turn that he knew to be at the end of the swift water would head them straight for it. The roar of the fire was now so loud as almost to drown the sound of the noisy rapids, and Shapian soon saw that it was to be a hard race, and a swift one, to gain the lake—and then there was the portage, and it was a long one.

The smoke was now so thick that when they neared the rapids they could not see fifty feet ahead of them, and Shapian had all he could do to find the place to enter it. Standing up in the canoe to get a better view, he at length found the starting point; and then with a swift rush they were into the dashing, boiling white water. Although he was hardly able to see through the smoke, Shapian skilfully picked his way down the crooked, difficult channel between the rocks. Great curling, hissing waves lashed out at the frail canoe, throwing it violently from one white-cap to another; dark, oily-looking swells gripped its under side like evil monsters seeking to pour in over the sides and sink it. Spinning eddies snatched wickedly at the paddles as the little craft leaped like a madly charging horse between the black, savage-looking rocks that lay in wait to rip and tear the light canoe to pieces.

And above the thunderous roar of the tumbling waters there came the duller, deeper, and terribly frightening sound of the oncoming fire. Smoke poured across the river in dense, whirling clouds, and through it sped the leaping canoe with its crew of three. And the sleeping passenger in the basket woke up, and excited by all the noise, and quite aware that something unusual was happening, began to take a part in the proceedings, and added his little thin voice to the uproar, though it could hardly be heard, and he rocked and shook his house of bark so violently that a moment had to be spared to lay a heavy bundle on it to keep it right side up.

Shapian strained and fought with his paddle and all of his young strength against the mighty power of the racing torrent, turning the canoe cleverly this way and that, swinging, sidling, and slipping from one piece of clear water to the next, checking the canoe in the quieter places while he stood up to get a better view of what lay ahead—and then away into the white water again. Meanwhile Sajo pulled and pushed and pryed on her paddle with might and main, as Shapian shouted to her above the rattle and the din 'Gyuk-anik' (to the right hand), or 'Mashk-anik' (to the left hand), or 'Wee-betch' (hurry), and sometimes 'Pae-ketch' (easy there). Sheets of spray flew from the sides of the canoe as it heaved and bounced and jerked, and some of it came in, and Sajo, who was in front, soon became soaked. Except that the smoke made the safe channel so hard to find, they were in no real danger from the rapids itself, for Shapian, like all his people, both young and old, was very skilful in a canoe and understood, even at his age, a great deal about the movements of water; and he had often run these rapids with his father. Sajo, trusting in him completely, laughed and cried out in her excitement, for this was like a show to her, and she let out little yelps as she had heard her father and the other Indians do, with their louder whoops and yells as they ran a dangerous piece of water—though she had always been left safely on the shore to watch. But Shapian, who knew how serious things really were, never made a sound besides his loud commands as captain of their little ship, and when he could spare an eye from the turmoil of madly boiling water all about him, gave anxious glances to the side from which the fire was coming. And coming it was—with the speed of a train, it seemed—rushing down the hills towards them like a crimson sea, with great roaring streamers of flame flying high above the burning forest. Once he looked back, to find that the fire had crossed the narrow lake behind them; now there was only one way to go—forward, though he said never a word to Sajo about it. The air, that had been thick with heavy rolls and banks of smoke, now commenced to turn darker and darker, and the light was dimmed till it appeared almost as though twilight had fallen, so early in the day, and hardly anything could be seen around them; and nothing seemed real any more, and they moved like people in a dream.

Desperately Shapian drove the canoe ahead, for well

he knew that if they were caught in this place they would be either burnt alive or suffocated. By now the portage was not very far, and beyond it lay the lake that they must get to—and get to fast!

They shot out from the foot of the rapids into a deep, still pool, and here they found themselves surrounded by strange moving shapes, dimly seen through the smoke-clouds, as on all sides all manner of animals were passing, tearing along the shore, or swimming through the pool, or splashing noisily along the shallows, by ones and twos, separately or in small groups, all headed for the big lake, the same one our own travellers were aiming for, each and every one making for the safety that he knew he would find there. Animals that seldom wetted their feet were swimming in the pool—squirrels, rabbits, woodchucks, and even porcupines. Deer leaped through or over the underbush, their white tails flashing, eyes wide with terror. A bear lumbered by at a swift, clumsy gallop, and a pair of wolves ran, easily and gracefully, beside a deer—their natural prey; but they never even looked at him. For none were enemies now; no one was hungry, or fierce, or afraid of another. And all the people of the woods, those that went on two legs and others that had four, and those with wings and some that swam, animals and birds and creeping things, creatures, some of them, that dared not meet at any other time, were now fleeing, side by side, from that most merciless of all their foes, dangerous and deadly alike to every one of them from the smallest to the greatest—the Red Enemy of the Wilderness, a forest fire.

Sajo, now realising what all this meant, became terror-stricken, and Shapian, almost in despair himself, yet knowing that their lives depended on him, kept his courage up and soothed her as best he could, and she paddled bravely on. But the forest that had always been their home, and had always seemed so friendly, had suddenly become a very terrible place to be in. It would have been so to any grown-up; yet these two children, one of them eleven and the other fourteen years of age, remember, kept their heads and fought like good soldiers for their lives, and for Chilawee's. And this same Chilawee was no great help, as you can well believe; on the contrary, he showed every sign of causing trouble and delay. Sensing real danger, as all animals do, and scared out of his wits by the sounds and scent of the other creatures that passed on every side, he was screeching at the top of his lungs and pounding and tearing at the lid of his prison, as it must now have seemed to him, and if some way were not found to quiet him, would soon be out of it; and once in the water he could never again be found in all this hurry and confusion.

A few short minutes and they were at the portage. The trail was nearly hidden by the blinding smoke, and down the slopes of the near-by ridge the hoarse roar of the fire was coming swiftly. The darkness that had fallen as the smoke poured over the forest was now lighted up by a terrible red glow, and the heat from it could be plainly felt. Quickly they threw their stuff ashore. Chilawee was now in such a state that he could never be carried in any other way except as a separate load. This landing being safe for the minute, and not knowing what shape things were in at the other end, they at once decided to leave him here, and it was but the work of a moment to turn the canoe over on top of the basket, so as to hold down the lid (like all his kind when very frightened, Chilawee forgot to use his teeth), and taking each a load the children started across, running at a dog-trot. On all sides thick moving coils of black and yellow smoke wound and billowed around them as they ran, and took strange shapes and forms and seemed to reach out with pale waving hands to hold them back, and through the whirling smoke-clouds the trees beside the trail loomed indistinct like tall, dark, silent ghosts; while here and there red eyes of flame glowed at them through the haze.

But they kept right on at their steady trot. At the far side there was a breeze from off the lake, and the end of the portage was clear. Gulping a few breaths of fresh air, they left their loads beside the water's edge and raced back for Chilawee and the canoe—I say 'raced', but the race was often little but a scramble as, gasping and half-blinded, they staggered down the trail, half the time with their eyes closed to relieve the pain in them, and to shut out the stinging, burning smoke, while they groped their way along, their hearts filled with a fear such as they had never before known. By the time they were back at the canoe, sparks and burning brands were falling everywhere, and the angry glow had deepened so that everything—trees, smoke, and water—was red with it. And now, close at hand, could be heard a dreadful low, rushing sound.

The fire was almost upon them.

And at the same time Chilawee, having made up his mind to save his own little life as best he could, was gnawing steadily away at the thin bark sides of his box; in no time at all he would be through. If only it would hold together for just five more minutes!

In a moment Shapian tore off his sister's head shawl, and quickly soaking it in water, with swift movements wrapped it about her head and face, leaving only her eyes and nose showing. Then splashing water over her clothes he said:

'Do not wait. I will come quickly. Go!!'

And hugging Chilawee's basket tight to her body with both arms, Sajo disappeared into that awful, glowing tunnel of a trail.

*   *   *   *   *   *

After he had seen his sister pass from sight, Shapian was delayed perhaps a full minute while he wetted his own clothes and slipped the paddles into the carrying-thongs. How he wished now for his father's guiding hand! He was doing the best he knew, with his small experience, to save the lives of all three of them, and he hoped he had chosen aright. And now Sajo was in there ahead of him, alone; he must hurry!

Throwing the canoe up, and over, with his head inside between the paddles, which formed a kind of yoke, he was quickly on his way. But in that short minute that he had been detained, the fire had gained on him, and while he ran as swiftly as a boy of fourteen could well do with a twelve-foot canoe on his shoulders, he saw, not far away to one side, a solid, crackling wall of flame. Trees fell crashing in the midst of it, and others burst with loud reports like gun-fire. Onward he tore through what had now become a cave of crimson smoke, half-choked, his eyes stinging, his head throbbing with the heat. But he clenched his teeth and kept on, while close beside him the blazing forest crackled, and thundered, and roared. Whole tree-tops caught fire with a rush and a horrible screeching, tearing sound, and flames leaped from tree to tree like fiery banners, ever nearer and nearer to the trail.

Beneath the canoe some clear air remained, which helped him a little, but the heat was all he could stand. Once a burning spruce tree came crashing down so near the portage that its flaming top fell across the trail ahead of him in a flurry of sparks and licking tongues of flame, and he was obliged to wait precious moments while the first fury of the burning brush died down; and then he jumped, with the canoe still on his shoulders, over the glowing trunk. The hot breath of it fanned his body and nearly choked him, and he stumbled to his knees as he landed. Righting himself, he cleared the canoe before the fire had harmed it.

On the upturned canoe fell large flakes of burning bark and red-hot ashes, that lay there and smoked and smouldered, so that to anyone who might have followed him, it must have seemed to be already burning, which, in very truth, it was not far from doing. And now he should have caught up to his sister; she would be slower than he, for the basket was an awkward affair to run with, whereas a bark canoe, though very much heavier, was a steady, well-balanced load, even for a boy. And he suddenly became terrified lest Chilawee had cut open his box and escaped on the way, and Sajo having delayed somewhere to capture him, that he had passed them. But just ahead the smoke was clearing, and he felt the wind from the lake. And then, sick and dizzy, his sight blurred by the water that streamed from his eyes, he stumbled again, and this time fell heavily, canoe and all, over something soft that lay in the pathway—there, face down across the trail, lay Sajo! And clutched tightly in one of her hands was the basket—empty. Chilawee had at last cut his way out, and was gone!

Hardly knowing what he was doing, Shapian crawled from under the canoe, lifted Sajo across his knees and scrambled, somehow, to his feet, and then, his breath coming in choking sobs, his knees bending under him and a great ringing in his ears he staggered with her in his arms to the lake shore.

Here he laid her down and threw water over her face, and rubbed her hands, and cried out, 'Sajo, Sajo, speak to me, speak!' And she opened her eyes and said faintly 'Chilawee'. And he dared not tell her there was no Chilawee any more, only an empty basket.

And now the smoke was rolling out over them even here; the whole portage was aflame, and waiting only to wet Sajo's shawl and throw it over her face, Shapian went back for the canoe. Fortunately it was not far, as, unable to lift it any more, he seized it by one end and dragged it to the water, stern out and bow inshore so as to load the quicker. Quickly he threw in the bundles, and lifted Sajo into the bow, while she held tightly to the basket and cried weakly, 'Chilawee, Chilawee, Chilawee', and moaned, and kept repeating 'Chilawee'.

All this took but a short time, and running lightly over the load to the other end, Shapian commenced to back the canoe out stern first, as fast as he was able; and a big sob came in his throat as he thought of their little furry friend who was now past all help, left behind. Yet surely, he thought, the little creature, gifted to find water easily, might have reached the lake, and even if lost might still be living—when behind him, from out on the lake, came the sound of a smart slap, and a splash upon the water, and there was the lost Chilawee, alive and quite well, thank you, giving out, by means of his tail, his private and personal opinion of this Red Enemy that he had so narrowly

'*There, face down across the trail, lay Sajo.*'

escaped. And Shapian shouted out in a great voice,
'Sajo! Sajo! Chilawee is safe, Chilawee is out on the
lake—look!'

And at that Sajo, lying there in the bow of the canoe,
burst into tears and sobbed as if her heart would break;
she would not cry before, when she believed her little
friend was dead, but now he was known to be safe she
was free to cry all she wanted, to cry as loud and as
long as she liked—with joy!

Chilawee was quite far out, and in no danger, but a
canoe does not start very quickly when paddled backwards, and being still in shallow water, was too close
to shore for safety; and at the edge of the forest, leaning
out over the water, was a huge pine tree that was
hollow, and had been burning fiercely all this time.
Shapian was still struggling to get the canoe backed
away far enough to turn it (and it did not take nearly
as long for all this to happen as it does to tell about it),
when the bark of the pine, dried out by the intense
heat, cracked wide open, and the hurrying tongue of
fire rushed up this channel as if it had been a stove-
pipe, to the top of it. The great fan-shaped head of the
towering tree, that had looked proudly out over the
wilderness for many a hundred years, burst into a mass
of flame that leaped into the air above it, the height
again of the tree itself. And then the burnt-out butt,
unable to stand against the force of the soaring flames,
gave way, and the mighty trunk tottered and began to
fall, outwards towards the lake, swayed a little side-

ways, and then started on its fiery path, straight for the canoe. Slowly at first, then faster and faster the hundred-foot giant overbalanced, and the terrible fan of flame rushed downwards. Real terror, for the first time, seized on Shapian, and with desperate strength he stopped the canoe and drove it smashing into the shore, while just behind him the burning tree plunged into the lake with a deafening crash, and a hissing and a screeching that could have been heard for a mile or more as the fire and water met. Smoke and steam poured up and smothered everything as the flames went out, so that Shapian could see nothing, and the waves from this terrific splash rocked the canoe violently, and Sajo, beside herself with fright, jumped to her feet in the dangerously rolling canoe and screamed, and screamed, and Shapian sprang over the side and ran through the water to her, and held her in his arms, and comforted her, and told her that there was nothing more to fear.

And out on the lake Master Chilawee slapped his little tail in small defiance. In a few short moments the canoe was away, this time without any accident, and the little beaver, seeming mighty glad that he was found again, gave himself up quite cheerfully, and was lifted by this so-impudent tail of his and dropped aboard, where he clambered around on the load, and smelled at the children, and ran about, and altogether showed signs of the greatest pleasure and excitement. He did not seem to have lost one single hair, no doubt because he ran so low to the ground on his short legs, so that everything passed over him; and so now he was celebrating, and they all had quite a reunion out there on the lake.

Before they had gone very far, Sajo began to feel better, and soon was well enough to sit up. Shapian would not let her paddle, and made her sit facing him, while she told her story, and related how, choked by the hot, burning smoke, and not being able to see, she had been unable to catch Chilawee when he fell from the basket, and had become confused and fallen, where, she did not know, and had then been unable to get up again. And that was all she knew about it until she found Shapian pouring water over her face. She did not remember calling Chilawee, though she knew he had run away, having seen him, as though in a dream, disappear into the clouds of smoke. And when she had finished her story, she began to look hard at her brother's face, and then commenced to laugh! And the more she looked the louder she laughed, and Shapian was a little frightened, and began to wonder if the dangers she had been through had touched her mind, until she exclaimed:

'Shapian!—your face—you should see it, why—you have no eyebrows!' And then suddenly she stopped laughing and felt for her own eyebrows, and asked anxiously. 'How are mine, are they all right?' and looked over the side of the canoe at the water to see the reflection of her face. But the canoe was moving, and ruffling the water, and she could, of course, see nothing, and now very alarmed she cried:

'Oh, stop the canoe so I can see—tell me, are my eyebrows there?'

And she got into a great way about it, and Shapian laughed at her, in his turn, and would not say; until at last he told her they were there all right, yes, both of them; which indeed they were, as her face had been covered most of the time. But it was just like a girl, said Shapian to himself, to worry about a little thing like eyebrows when they had all so nearly lost their lives.

That afternoon they made an early camp, in a good safe place, on an island far out on the lake, and here they looked over the damage. Shapian could not very well repair his eyebrows, which would grow out later of their own accord, but he had plenty to do with the canoe.

The hard smash the bow had got against the shore when they had dodged the falling tree had torn off a good-sized strip of bark; the spruce gum at the seams had melted, and the burning embers that had fallen on it had smouldered long enough to scorch a number of pretty thin places in the sides and bottom. Also their tent and blankets had a few holes burnt in them by flying sparks. But the loss was quite small considering, and they could easily have fared a great deal worse. The top was gone off Chilawee's box, and it had a hole the size of a quart measure in the side of it (Chilawee's part in the battle!). But there were plenty of birch trees around, and Shapian cut sheets of bark from them, and sewed a patch on the hole and made another lid that fitted nearly as well as the old one, and he fixed up the canoe with a few patches and some fresh gum. Sajo, meanwhile, busied herself with needle and thread which no Indian girl or woman will travel very far without, and soon had the tent and blankets serviceable again, and by the time darkness fell, everything was in readiness for a new start in the morning.

CHAPTER THREE

The Little Prisoner

AND meanwhile, what of Chikanee?

We must go back to the day the trader walked out of Gitchie Meegwon's camp with him, right out of the lives of his friends, it seemed, for ever.

During the four or five days it took the trader, with his Ojibway canoe-men, to make the journey back to Rabbit Portage, Chikanee did not fare so badly, as one of the Indians took good care of him, keeping him well supplied with food and water. But he could not understand why Chilawee was not with him, and wondered where Sajo and Shapian had disappeared to. And he began to be lonesome for them all, and often cried out for Sajo to come to him, as she had always done when she heard the little beaver calling. But no one came except the stranger Indian, and then only to change his water and to give him food. This man, by the trader's orders, accompanied Chikanee on the steamboat to see that he arrived safely at the railroad, and there left him; the money for him was paid over to the Indian, and what happened to him now did not greatly matter.

Having now come to a stop, and thinking that he must be home again, he wailed loudly for liberty and recognition, expecting his playmates to come and take him out of this stuffy and uncomfortable box. But none came. So he started to chew at the box, and strange, harsh voices spoke angrily to him. He next tried to climb the walls of his prison, but they were too high, and these strangers shouted at him, and pounded on the box to keep him quiet, and now, thoroughly frightened, he lay still, whimpering and lonely.

A little later he was loaded on to a train that thundered and roared its way for many hours. When the train first started the noise drove him nearly crazy, and in his terror he tried to dive to freedom through his tiny dish of water, and upset it; so that, besides his other misery, he soon began to suffer from thirst. He had been snatched away from home too hurriedly for Sajo to have time to drop a bannock in the box, which would have lasted him several days, and no one now thought of providing him with anything to eat. And so, sick, hungry, lonesome, and wild with fear, he started desperately to cut his way out of the crate. In this he would have quickly succeeded, but striking a nail he broke one of his four cutting teeth, which made gnawing too painful to continue. His bedding, what little there was of it, became dirty, and the motion of the train thumped and bumped him against the hard sides of the box, so that he became bruised and sore. He tried hard to stay in the centre, away from the walls of his prison, but never could. One of the trainmen, intending to be kind, threw to him some crusts of bread from his own lunch, but he thought that the little beaver's frantic clutchings at his hands was a sign of ill-temper, and from then on they were afraid of him— so small a little creature to be afraid of!—and no one attempted to give him any more bedding or food, and his water-dish remained empty for the same reason.

And he raised his voice in cries of misery and called and called for his small companions, who now could never hear him, wailed in his child-like voice for them to come and take away this great trouble that had befallen him. But no one paid any attention, if they ever even heard him, drowned as was his feeble outcry by the roar of the train.

At length, after many stops and starts, each of which jolted and slammed him from one hard side of his prison to the other, and a last, and cruelly rough ride in a delivery van, there came a sudden quietness. The cleats were taken from across the top of the box with a frightful screeching as the nails were drawn, and he was lifted out by a hand that held him very firmly by the tail; a large, strong hand, yet somehow a very gentle one. Then the other hand came up and was held against his chest as he hung head down, bringing him right end up, and a finger rubbed gently on one hot, tired little paw, and a deep voice spoke soothing words; so that suddenly he felt rather comfortable. For this man was a keeper of animals, and attendant in the Park where Chikanee was to stay, and he knew his business very well. And when he examined his small captive, and saw how miserable, and bedraggled, and covered with

dirt the little creature was—he who had been so proud
and careful of his coat!—the keeper said angrily to the
delivery man (who, poor fellow, was not to blame at
all):

'No water, nothing to eat, dry feet, dry tail, dry
nose, teeth all broken up; if that isn't a shame, nothing
ever was. Some way to ship a beaver, I'll say! But
we'll soon fix you up, old-timer.' For the man had
been expecting his little guest, having had a letter
about him, and had everything ready to receive him,
and Chikanee soon found himself in an enclosure built
of something like stone, but not nearly as friendly as
stone, and surrounded by a rail of iron bars.

And in this gaol of iron and concrete Chikanee, for
no crime at all, was to spend the rest of his days.

Chikanee, gentle, lovable Chikanee, was now supposed to be a wild and probably dangerous beast!

It was not a very large place, a mere hutch after the
freedom of the big lake beside which he had spent
most of his short life, but that did not matter for the
moment—he smelled water! And then he saw, right
in front of him, a deep, clear pool; not a very big one,
to be sure, but at least it was water. Into this he
immediately threw himself and drank thirstily, floating
on the surface, while the cracked and dried-out tail
and feet soaked up the life-giving moisture, and the
cakes of dirt loosened and washed from off him as he
swam slowly back and forth. This seemed like the
beavers' heaven itself, after more than three days of

noise, starvation, dirt and utter misery, and the hot, fevered little body cooled off and all the bumps and bruises ceased to throb, as the cool water slowly got in its good work on him.

And now, he thought, this must be just the plunge-hole. Down there, somewhere, lay the entrance, and through this he would set out and would, no doubt, come to his home-lake, there to find his playmates on the shore; and then Chilawee would run to welcome him and roll on his woolly back with joy, and Sajo would come and pick him up, and hug him and make much of him, and whisper in his ear, and tickle him in that funny place under his chin, and all these hard times would be forgotten.

So, with a great splurge he dived straight down—to strike his head on the hard bottom of the pool, almost stunning himself. Again he tried, with the same result. He scratched and bit at the concrete, thinking to tear his way through it to the tunnel that must, somewhere, lead out of it. But he only cracked and split his claws and took more chips out of his remaining teeth. Then he scrambled out of the pool and over to the bars, and tried to squeeze through them; but they were too close together. He tried to gnaw at them, but his broken teeth never even scratched them. So he ran round and round inside the enclosure, stopping here and there to dig, but to no purpose. For a long time he worked, running back to the pool and out again to the bars, trying to gnaw, trying to dig; but it was useless. And then at last he realised that there was no opening anywhere, no plunge-hole, no escape; and weary, wretched and hopeless, he lay flat on the hard, hot floor of the pen and moaned, moaned as he had done when Sajo had nursed him to sleep whenever he had been lonesome—only then he had moaned with joy, and now it was from misery.

The attendant stood by for a long time, and watched and shook his head, and said, 'Too bad, little fellow, too bad'. This was his job, taming these wild creatures that were sent to him from time to time; yet, liking animals as he did, he sometimes hated the work. And he pitied the little beaver that was struggling so helplessly to be free, for this was not the first one that had come under his care, and he knew their gentle nature. And stepping in through the gate of the pen, he picked up Chikanee carefully and cleverly, so that, as in the first place, he was not scared or excited, but was actually comfortable in his hands—they were so much more friendly than the concrete!

The keeper carried Chikanee to his cottage, which was close by, inside the Park. He had three young children, and when they saw their father bringing in a little beaver, they crowded round to see, and they shouted and clapped their hands with glee, so that Chikanee was afraid again, and tried to burrow into the man's coat; for already he had begun to trust him. And their father quieted the young ones and set the little creature on the floor, where, finding himself once more in a house, he felt a little more at home than in the cage. They all stood watching to see what he would do, and the keeper's wife said:

'The wee mite! Look how thin he is!—Joey,' to one of the youngsters, 'go get an apple; those other beavers we used to have were just crazy for apples.'

So this Joey fellow went and got one right away, and put it down on the floor in front of Chikanee. He had never seen an apple before, but he sniffed at it, and oh! what a wonderful smell came from it! And so he cut into it as best he could with his poor wee broken teeth and then, what a taste!—the most delicious taste in all the world! And seizing hold of this wonderful titbit with both hands, he demolished nearly the half of it. At this the keeper was very pleased, for some of his prisoners refused all food, and died, but now he knew that this one would recover; somehow he had been none too sure about it. And the delighted children laughed to see him sitting up there like a little man while he ate, and the keeper's wife exclaimed:

'There, didn't I tell you? He'll be all right in no time.'

Then the man brought in the sprays of fresh, juicy poplar leaves he had placed in the pen for him, but which he had not touched. But now he ate them, and the children wondered to see him holding the leaves in little bunches in his hands while he put them in his mouth. Feeling a good deal better by now, he made small sounds of pleasure while he ate, and at that the

young ones marvelled even more, and one, a little girl
with golden hair and a round, rosy face, said:

'Listen, listen to him talk, just like a little, wee baby.
O daddy, do let's keep him in the kitchen!' And their
mother spoke up too: 'Yes, Alec, let's keep him here
for a spell; there's no one in the Park—it's almost like
putting a child in prison.' And Alec answered:

'Perhaps you're right. We'll fix him a place in here
for to-night.'

So they made a place for our Chikanee in the kitchen,
and Alec the keeper fastened a low, wide pan of water
to the floor, and set a large box down on its side, with
plenty of clean straw in it for a bed for him. And
there the little beaver spent the night, not happily
perhaps, but very comfortably.

The next morning Alec returned him to the pen, so
that any of the public who came to the Park could see
him; but when evening came round again and the
grounds were empty, the keeper brought him back to
the cottage. And from then on he did this every day,
and Chikanee spent all the hours when he was not
'working' in the keeper's house, and in the kitchen had
his bed, and his big pan of water, and ate his leaves
and twigs there. And each day he had a nice, juicy
apple, which quite made up for a lot of his troubles,
though not for all of them. Every morning there was a
considerable mess to clean up, of peeled sticks, and cut
branches, and left-over leaves, and the floor was all
slopped up with water, but the children willingly

'Feeling a good deal better by now, he made small sounds of pleasure while he ate.'

turned to and cleaned up, after he was carried away to his daily task of being stared at in the cage. Nobody seemed to mind the little trouble he was. He got along famously with the family and, in his own small way, soon became quite a part of the household.

As time went on he got to know them all, and he would romp clumsily with the youngsters; and to them he was a kind of tumbling, good-natured toy, a good deal like one of those roguish wool puppies to be found on Christmas trees. But to Chikanee, it could never be the same as it had been at O-pee-pee-soway, and often he didn't want to play, but lay quietly in his box, his little heart filled with a great empty longing for his old playmates.

Before very long his teeth had grown in, and he spent a lot of time sharpening them against one another, grinding and rattling them together at a great rate. His coat, which he had sadly neglected for a time, so that it had become all tangled and awry, now got its daily scrubbing and combing, and his small frame, that had for a while been little more than a bag of bones, soon filled out, and he began to look like the old Chikanee again. And in a way he was happy; but never quite.

While in the cage he was really miserable, and the keeper knew this, and always felt badly when he put the little fellow in there each morning, and looked back at this pitiful little creature that gazed after him so wistfully as he walked away, sitting there alone on the bare cement floor, surrounded by bars that would have held a grizzly bear. He remembered that a beaver may live more than twenty years—twenty years in that prison of iron and concrete! In twenty years his own family would be grown up and away from there; he himself might be gone. The town would have become a great city (it was not really a very big place); people would come and go—free people, happy people—and through it all, this unhappy little beast, who had done no harm to anyone, and seemed only to want someone to be kind to him, would, for twenty long and lonely years, look out through the bars of that wretched pen as though he had been some violent criminal; waiting for the freedom that would never be his, waiting only to die at last. And, thought the keeper, for no good reason at all, except that a few thoughtless people, who never really cared if they ever saw a beaver, might stare for a minute or two at the disconsolate little prisoner, and then go away and forget they had ever seen him. Somehow it did not seem fair, to this kind-hearted man, and when he watched the little creature rollicking with the children in his funny, clumsy way, he wished very much that there was something that he could do about it, and decided to make his small prisoner as happy as he could, and give him the freedom of the cottage as long as it was at all possible.

CHAPTER FOUR

The Prisoner Released

Two days' more travelling brought Sajo and Shapian to Rabbit Portage, the trading station. They made camp nearby, and then Shapian set off to see the trader who had bought Chikanee. But the trader would not help: the beaver had been bought for fifty dollars for a Zoo in the Big City many miles away. Poor Shapian had never heard of so much money, but he bravely offered to sell his gun, and to work ever so hard to earn enough to buy back Chikanee. It was no good; the trader was very firm; it was a business affair, and had been settled once and for all.

Shapian did not know how to break the news to his sister, but in his despair a friend came to his help. A missionary wondered who the two Indian children were, and as he was so friendly to them, they told him all their story, and, of course, Chilawee came along too to play his part.

The missionary was poor, so he could not give them the money needed, but he had a good idea. He called a meeting of all the folk at Rabbit Portage, and told them the story of the children and their beavers. Everyone wanted to help, so a collection was made, and this proved enough for the railway journey with a little over. The missionary bought the tickets, and gave Shapian the few dollars left; these the boy put into a little bag which he hung by a cord round his neck for safety.

Then the missionary wrote a letter to some friends in the

Big City who would look after the children. He wrote the address on the envelope and told Shapian to ask a policeman to show them the way to the house. The Indian boy had never seen a policeman, but he kept saying 'poliss-man' to himself so that he should not forget the name.

The next morning everyone came along to see Sajo, Shapian and Chilawee off; there was much waving of handkerchiefs and many cries of good wishes as the train puffed out of the station.

WHEN the train on which Sajo, Shapian, and their small fellow-traveller Chilawee were riding made the last of its many stops and came to a standstill in the city station, the children were almost too scared to get off. The guard, who had had his eye on them all the way, helped them out, spoke a few words of encouragement, and left them to attend to his other duties.

They found themselves in a world of noise. The hurrying throngs of people, the hiss of escaping steam, the clang of engine bells, the shriek of whistles and the thunderous bellowing of starting and stopping loco-motives, deafened and terrified them, and they stood hand in hand on the platform, not knowing which way to turn and not daring to move. Before, behind, and on every side of them was a terrific confusion and a ceaseless din. Lorries piled high with baggage of every kind rumbled by, and one of these came straight for them, and Shapian pulled his sister aside only just in time to escape being run over by it. The station was, to them, a vast, echoing cave filled with terrifying sights and sounds, and never before had they felt so small and defenceless. They felt more alone here, in the midst of all these people, than they had ever done in the forest, with its silence and its quiet, peaceful trees. People looked at them curiously as they passed, but everyone seemed to be too busy rushing this way and that to pay much attention to them.

So there they stood, in all that deafening uproar, two little people from the Silent Places, as scared and bewildered, and nearly as helpless, as the two tiny kitten-beavers had been when Gitchie Meegwon found them. Yet Sajo, with all her fear, had only one thought —Chikanee had come through all this *alone*! While Shapian began to wish himself back in the forest fire again, amongst the friendly animals, Chilawee, for his part, closed his ears as tight as two tiny black purses and lay perfectly still, jammed tight into a corner of his basket.

They had been standing there for what seemed to them an hour (though it had really been only a few moments), and Shapian was thinking of making *some* kind of move towards a huge door through which crowds of people were flowing like a swift, rushing river, when there stopped in front of them a young boy. He was about Shapian's own age, and was dressed in a neat, red uniform with bright buttons all down the front of his short, tightly fitting coat, and on the side of his head there was a little hat that looked more like a very small, round box than anything else.

'Hullo, you kids,' he said cheerfully. 'Are you lost? Who are you looking for?'

Poor Shapian, confronted by this self-possessed and magnificent-looking personage, never before having seen a page boy, found that he had completely forgotten any English he ever knew, and could remember only one word; so he said it.

'Poliss-man,' he stammered nervously.

'You want a policeman, eh?' said the page, who was a smart lad and got to the point at once. 'O.K. Come along with me.' And beckoning to them he set off at a great pace, his shiny boot-heels tapping sharply on the hard platform. The little Indians, silent-footed in their mocassins, slipped softly along behind him, though they almost had to trot to keep up, Shapian carrying Chilawee's basket in one hand and holding tightly on to his sister with the other. It must have been a queer-looking procession. Their guide steered them through the crowds, over to the entrance and down a great hall filled with more people (nearly all the people in the world, thought Shapian), and brought them over to a big, stout man who stood beside a door at the far end. He also had a number of bright buttons on his coat.

'Hey, Pat,' the page called to him. 'Here's a couple of kids want to see a policeman', and pushed them forward, continuing—rather disrespectfully, I fear— 'You shouldn't be hard to see, you're big enough. Look like Indians to me—better watch your scalp!'

And with an impudent grin at the police officer and a wink at the children, he dodged into the crowd and disappeared.

'Oho,' exclaimed the policeman loudly, looking down on the two youngsters, with his hands behind his back. 'Oho, so it's scalps, is it?' said he, looking very fiercely at them, as though he were about to take them prisoner—though his eyes had an odd twinkle about them and were pleasantly crinkled at the corners. ''Tis young Injuns yez are, eh? The little craytures! Well, 'tis a mighty poor scalp ye'll get from me, that's been bald as an egg this twenty years; and well did the little imp know it that brought ye here!'

Although he talked so fiercely, his face was round and jolly, and he wore his helmet a little to one side of his head in rather a jaunty sort of fashion, as though being a policeman was the most entertaining business imaginable. But seeing that the 'little craytures' were becoming alarmed, he asked, in what he considered to be a lower voice:

'And what can I be doin' for ye?'

'You—poliss-man?' asked Shapian timidly.

'Yes, me lad,' answered the constable, putting his helmet just a trifle more to one side, 'I'm a policeman, and a good one—and where would ye be wantin' to go?'

Shapian, along with his English, had quite forgotten the letter the missionary had given him, but now remembering one, he thought of the other, and pulling

it out gave it to the officer, who read the address on the
envelope and said:

'I see. I'm on dooty and cannot leave; but set ye
down and wait, and I'll take ye there. And it's Patrick
O'Reilly himself will see that no harrm comes to yez.'

And so our two young wanderers, feeling a good
deal more at their ease, sat on the end of a long row of
seats and waited. And the big policeman, who seemed
to be in such continual good humour over nothing at
all, asked them a number of questions, and Shapian,
having got his English into pretty fair working order
by now, told him most of the story. And the jolly
Irishman became quite depressed about it, and said
that he—Patrick O'Reilly himself, mind you—would
take them to the people who owned the Park.

*   *   *   *   *   *

*And the friendly 'poliss-man' was as good as his word, for
when he came off duty, he took them along to a restaurant and
gave them a good meal. It was all very strange to Sajo and
Shapian, and they were really rather frightened, but the thought
that they were near Chikanee gave them courage. After the
meal—and Chilawee had his share too—the policeman took
them off to the address which the missionary had written on the
envelope. There they were to stop the night, and their new
friend said he would call for them in the morning. They were
much too excited to sleep.*

*   *   *   *   *   *

Early the following day, Patrick O'Reilly called for
his charges, as he had promised. But they did not go

right away to the animal Park as they had expected, but to a large building in the city, where the Park owners had an office.

Afraid that at the last moment some accident might happen to the money, Shapian often felt at the lump under his shirt, where the little bag was; they were going to need it very soon now, and he was getting nervous. In the other hand he carried Chilawee in his basket, and beside him, never more than three feet away, Sajo walked with short, little-girl steps, her shawl wrapped about her head and shoulders.

There was a swift ride in an elevator, which they far from enjoyed, and then they found themselves, with the Irishman beside them, standing before a desk behind which sat a man.

And this was the man in whose hands was the fate of their little lost friend.

Sajo, who up till now had had such faith in her dream, became suddenly fearful and anxious, and trembled like a leaf. She had no idea what they were going to do if their offer was refused, and now that the moment had arrived she wanted to scream and run away. But she stood her ground bravely, determined to see it through, no matter what happened.

The man behind the desk was a youngish man with a pale, narrow face and a weak-looking chin. He had a cigarette in the corner of his mouth, burnt almost down to his lips, and one of his eyes was screwed up unpleasantly, to keep the smoke out of it, while he looked around with the other, so that at times he appeared cross-eyed. He spoke without removing the cigarette, squinting sharply at them with the eye that was in working order; and a very colourless, unfriendly looking eye it was.

'Well, what do you want?' he asked shortly.

There was a moment's silence, a very heavy, thick kind of a silence. I think that Sajo and Shapian had even stopped breathing. Then:

'Sorr,' commenced Pat the policeman, 'I telephoned Mr H—— last night concerning me young friends there, and we were all to meet him here, to talk over a small matter of business, belike—'

'You can do your business with me,' broke in the young man, in no very civil tone; 'Mr H—— is busy at present.' And he glanced towards a door that led into another room, which stood slightly open.

'You see, 'tis this way,' began Pat once more, when the young man looked at his wrist watch and interrupted again:

'Make it snappy, constable; I'm busy this morning.'

Pat got a little red in the face, and again started his speech, this time successfully. It was a speech that he had carefully rehearsed the night before, the story that, as he had said at the railroad station, was going to 'bring tears to the eyes of a heart of stone'. Evidently the young man did not have a heart of stone, however, for there were no tears; in fact, while Pat was talking, this impatient personage looked several times at his wrist watch, and lit a fresh cigarette from the stump in his mouth. Far from having a heart of stone, it began to look very much as though he had no heart at all. And the honest policeman became a little discouraged towards the last, and finished his tale rather lamely.

'...so the young people wants to buy the little baste back from ye: and I'll be so bold as to say that I think ye'll be doin' the Lord's own wurrk if ye let them have it.' And having done his best he stood there, nervously wiping his face with the big red handkerchief. The man straightened some papers on the desk and leaned back in his chair.

'Are you quite done?' he enquired coldly.

'Yes,' answered Pat, none too happily, for he began to fear, and with good reason, that he had lost the battle already.

'Oh,' said the clerk, 'thank you. Well, let me tell you'—his words fell like chips of ice on a plate of glass—'that beaver was bought in a fair and perfectly business-like way, and not from these ragamuffins at all, but from a reputable trader. We paid fifty dollars for him, which was a great deal more than the little brute was worth, and we have no intention of selling him back—unless we can get a good profit on the deal, and'—here he looked at the two little Indians—'I don't think your red-skinned *friends*, as you call them, are very well off judging by their looks.'

Pat turned redder than ever, but shrewdly suspecting

that money alone could talk to this hard-headed fellow, he pushed Shapian forward.

'Money,' he whispered hoarsely, 'that money. Money, give it now!' And Shapian, sick with fear, for he had understood nearly everything, stepped forward, fumbled for a moment in the pouch, and dropped his little wad of money on the desk.

The clerk took it, counted it. He sniffed:

'There's only fourteen dollars here.' He handed it back. 'Nothing doing,' he said, and to make sure that everybody understood he added, for good measure, 'All washed up; no sale; no good; no! Get me?'

They got him; everyone of them.

Nobody spoke, nobody moved; but to Shapian it was the end of the world—but no—was this true? And then the silence seemed suddenly to be choking him; the white face of the man behind the desk was getting bigger and bigger, was rushing towards him—the floor seemed to be going from under his feet—was he going to fall like a woman, faint, like a weak girl! He closed his eyes to shut out the sight of that pale, weak face with its one eye that leered at him so mockingly; he gritted his teeth, clenched his fists, and stiffened his young body upright in his old, proud way; and the dizzy feeling passed, leaving him cold and trembling.

And Sajo? She had been watching every move with painful eagerness, her eyes flitting from face to face like two frightened birds in a cage; and she had seen. No one needed to tell her.

They had failed. In just two minutes they had failed.

She came softly over beside Shapian, 'I know, my brother,' she said very quietly, in such a strange little voice that Shapian looked at her quickly, and put his arm about her, while she stood close, looking up at him, 'I know now. He is not going to give us Chikanee. I was wrong—about my dream. We have come to the city not to get Chikanee, after all. I think—perhaps—it was—to bring Chilawee to him. That must be what the Waterfall meant; so they could be together—so they won't be lonesome any more. That must be it. So—'

And her childish voice fell to a whisper, and the little dark head drooped. 'Tell this man—I give him—Chilawee—too.'

And she set Chilawee's basket upon the desk and stepped back, her face like a sheet of paper, her lips pale, and her eyes wide and dry, staring at the basket.

'What's this?' exclaimed the clerk, becoming angry. And Shapian told him:

''Nother beaver, Chilawee. His brother, that Chikanee, very lonesome. You keep him Chilawee too; not be lonesome then. Those are words of my sister. Me—' His voice stuck in his throat, and he couldn't say any more.

'Well, now,' said the clerk, smiling for the first time, though the smile improved his features very little. 'That's a horse of a different colour! We'll fix that up very quickly', and he reached for his pen—

'NO!!' suddenly shouted the policeman in a terrific voice, bringing his fist down on the desk with a crash, so that everybody jumped, and the ink-bottles and paper-weights and the pens and the pencils all jumped, and even the pale young man jumped, and turned a shade paler and his cigarette jumped from his lips to the floor.

'No, you don't,' bellowed Pat in a tremendous voice. 'No son of an O'Reilly will stand by and see a couple of helpless kids bullyragged and put upon by ye, nor the likes o' ye. Ye're a black-hearted scoundrel,' he roared, 'An' I'm an officer of the law, an' I'll arrest ye for conspiracy, an' fraud, an' misdemeanour, an' high-way robbery, an' assault, an'—' Here he ran out of the more attractive-sounding crimes, and growling fiercely started round the desk towards the now badly scared young man, who was backing away as hastily as possible in the direction of the other room, while Sajo and Shapian stood by with eyes as big as saucers. Just what this rather violent son of the O'Reillys intended to do, never became known, for at that moment the other door opened, and the fleeing young man found his line of retreat cut off, as he stumbled backwards into yet another guest to the party, and a voice, a very quiet, low voice said, 'Pardon me', as there appeared just inside the room a slim, grey-haired old gentleman, who stood peering over his spectacles at this astonishing scene.

He gave a slight cough, and said again, 'Pardon me,

if I appear to intrude', and then, very politely, 'Won't you sit down?'

Pat still snorted angrily and glared at his intended prisoner, who was not at all sure if he *hadn't* committed some crime or another, so that his hands trembled a little as he fumbled with a new cigarette.

'Pray sit down, gentlemen,' again invited the grey-haired man.

They sat down; somehow you felt that you must do as this mild-mannered old gentleman asked you. And he it was that owned the Park; it was Mr H—— himself.

'Now, let us talk matters over,' he suggested, looking from the policeman to the clerk, then to the children and back to the policeman again. 'Now, constable, on the telephone last night I promised to hear these children's story, and to consider what should be done. I have heard everything—from the other room, far better than if I had been here; for then certain things *did* happen, that would not otherwise have done so. I had already learned from you how far they have come, and what hardships and dangers they have been through to try and regain their pet. But I had to be careful; I had to know that it was not a fraud, and as I cannot understand their language, I wanted to see what they would do, before I could even consider the matter. Now I know the *whole* story, and I see that matters are going to be very difficult—for me.'

At this, the clerk looked around with a pleased expression, as if to say, 'There now, didn't I tell you?'

Mr H—— looked around too, tapping his spectacles on his knee:

'Everyone is listening, I hope?' he continued. 'Very good. Now, I heard these Indian children offer to give up their other pet, so the two little animals could be together, which proves to me their truthfulness. But, there is my side to be thought of. As George, here, says, it was a perfectly proper piece of business, and it cost me quite a sum of money. I cannot decide all at once. Moreover, it is not good for people, especially young people, for them to have everything they ask for—not, that is, unless they have worked for it.' And he looked at them a trifle severely through his glasses.

'But what are ye goin' to do about it, Sorr?' asked Pat, nearly exploding with impatience.

'Do?' queried this exasperating old man. 'Do? Oh, yes; I think I have decided what to do—just this!' And taking Chilawee's basket he beckoned the children over. 'There,' he said gently, 'there is your small friend. Now'—and becoming all at once very brisk and business-like, he wrote something on a card and handed it to Pat—'and now, go down to the Park with Mr O'Reilly, *and get the other one*. He is yours; you most certainly have earned him.'

Shapian stared, his mouth open—did he hear aright? Or was this another one of Sajo's dreams in which he had become entangled? Or perhaps it was one of his own!

*   *   *   *   *   *

I greatly doubt if either Sajo or Shapian remembered very much about that trip to the amusement park, up to the time that Pat pointed out the entrance that could now be seen not far ahead of them. Then Sajo started to run. She was not pale now, and her eyes, that had been so dry and staring, were all aglow. Her shawl fell back unheeded, and her braids flew out and bobbed up and down on her shoulders, as her little moccasined feet pattered on the pavement. Behind her came Shapian, unable to keep up with her on account of carrying the basket, inside which Chilawee, tired of being cooped up for so long, was making a great uproar. Next came the stalwart Mr O'Reilly, very red in the face, his helmet off, dabbing with his large red handkerchief at the head that had been 'bald as an egg for twenty years', puffing and blowing like a tug-boat that had a light touch of asthma.

Once he bellowed, 'Hey! What is this, a race?' But the youngsters kept going right on, and it is very doubtful if they ever heard him; so he fell to grumbling, 'The little haythens, they'll be the death of me yet, so they will.' But he kept valiantly on.

Several passers-by stopped to look at the young Indians in their forest clothes, racing along the street with the policeman apparently chasing them. They heard, too, the shrill cries and wails coming out of the basket, as Chilawee objected loudly to the shaking up he was getting in all this hurry; so a few of them turned and joined this strange parade, and followed this small, running, black-haired girl.

And behind them all—far, far behind—there came another person: a tall, brown-skinned man who strode along so softly, yet so swiftly through the city streets. And he looked so dark and stern that people were glad to step aside and let him pass, and stared after him and said to one another. 'Who is that? What kind of a man is that?' But he never so much as glanced at any one of them.

There was some delay at the entrance, as the Park was not yet open for the day, but O'Reilly soon caught up, and showed his card, and they were let in. Quite a respectable crowd had gathered, and pushed in with them as soon as the gates were opened. The attendant, who was none other than our friend Alec the keeper, already knew what to do, as Mr H—— had decided, at the last moment, to come too, and had given his orders and now stood in the crowd. At a nod from Mr H——, the keeper led Sajo quickly over towards the beavers' pen. And all at once she was pale as a ghost again. She seemed to be running in a great empty space at the end of which, miles away, was a dark, ugly-looking row of iron bars, and now, now—she could see through them, and there—yes, there was a brown, furry little animal sitting up in the centre of them, and—oh! was it?—could it be?—yes, it was—Chikanee!

And Sajo, no longer shy, forgot the watching people, forgot the noisy city, forgot everything but the small furry body that was now so close, and rushing to the iron fence she threw herself on her knees in the gravel, thrust her two arms through the bars, and screamed 'Chikanee! CHIKANEE!! CHIKANEE!!!'

The little beaver, not believing, sat without a move, looking.

'It's me, Sajo. Oh, Chikanee!' The cry was almost a wail. Oh, had he forgotten?

For a moment longer the little creature stood there, stock still, his chubby brown head cocked to one side, listening, as Sajo cried out again:

'*Chik-a-nee-e-e-e!!!*'—and then he knew. And with a funny little noise in his throat, he scrambled, as fast as his short legs would carry him, to the bars.

At that a little cheer broke out amongst the crowd, and there was a small commotion. And Alec the keeper now came forward and opened a small iron gate, and said, 'This way, Miss—a—Mam'selle—a—Senorita—' for he didn't quite know how he should address her, and was rather excited himself. And she rushed in, and kneeling down gathered the so-long-lost Chikanee up on her lap and bent over him; and they both were very still. And the gay head-shawl hid everything; and neither you, nor I, nor anyone else will ever know just what passed between those two on that fateful, that glorious, that never-to-be-forgotten morning.

And the grey-haired Mr H—— took his handkerchief from his pocket and blew his nose rather loudly; and Alec the keeper had suddenly become troubled with a cough. 'Humph,' he said, 'hurrumph.'

'You bet,' exclaimed Pat the policeman in a hearty

*'"It's me, Sajo. Oh, Chikanee!" The cry was almost
a wail. Oh, had he forgotten?'*

voice, although the keeper hadn't really said anything at all.

And now was to come the biggest thrill of all. Chilawee and Chikanee were to have *their* party now. They were only ten feet apart, and didn't know it! What a thrill was there!

So it was with wildly beating heart that Sajo and Shapian carried the basket in (one of them alone could never have handled this affair; it took the two of them to pull off the lid, they were in such a state); and they lifted Chilawee out, and set him down facing Chikanee, a short distance away. Then they stood and watched, breathlessly. For a second or two neither of the kittens moved, just stared at each other. Then, the truth slowly dawning in the little twilight minds, they crept towards one another, eyes almost starting out of their heads, ears wide open, listening, sniffing, creeping slowly forward until the creep became a walk, and the walk became a little shuffling trot, and now, sure at last that they had found each other, the trot broke suddenly into a gallop, and with a rush they met, head-on. And so violent was the collision, in a mild way of speaking, that, not being able to go any farther ahead, they went straight up on end, and with loud shrill cries they grasped each other tightly, and there, in front of all those people, began to wrestle!

The ceaseless, hopeless searching, the daily disappointments, all the misery and longing, the dreary empty nights of lonesomeness were over.

Big Small and Little Small were together again.

Before long they were disporting themselves all over the enclosure, and what had been a grim and ugly prison had now become a playground, the best use that it had ever yet been put to, I'll guarantee! And the children clapped their hands, and shouted and laughed and hallooed at them excitedly, while the wrestlers, or dancers, or whatever you have a mind to call them, stepped around in high feather, enjoying to the utmost what must have been to them the greatest moment in all their lives, up to that time and perhaps for ever after. Never before had they given quite such a brilliant performance; and the people cheered them on, and laughed, and the grey-haired Mr H—— waved his handkerchief quite furiously in the air, and I am not at all sure that he didn't shout a little himself.

Mr O'Reilly, just about dying to take a part in this happy occasion which he had helped so much to bring about, and very proud to think that he was the only one present who knew the whole story, appointed himself Master of Ceremonies, and while he performed his duties as a policeman and kept back the crowd, he also played the part of a modern radio announcer, and explained to them what it was all about, and cracked jokes, and beamed around on everybody in the most amiable fashion, and otherwise enjoyed himself immensely. And he ended up by declaring for all to hear:

'Well, I'm seein' it, but, bejapers, I'll never believe it.'

And then, having been there, watching, for quite some time—for he had not wished to interrupt this little celebration—there now came out from behind the people another figure—a tall dark man in moccasins. He was the same man who, a short time before, had been seen striding so swiftly through the city streets in this direction. A quietness fell upon the wondering crowd as he stepped forward. But Sajo and Shapian, busy with their playfellows, never noticed him until a voice, *the* voice, the one they knew so very well, said softly there behind them, in the quiet, musical language of the Ojibways:

'O-way, the clouds have indeed gone from off the face of the sun. Now my sorrow has gone too, melted away like the mists of early morning. These people have done much—very much—for us, my children. Let us now thank them.

'My son, my daughter, take up your Nitchie-keewense, your Little Brothers.

'O-pee-pee-soway is waiting.'

Big Feather had come to take them, all four of them, back to the Place of Talking Waters, to the Land of the North-West Wind.

And Sajo's dream had, after all, come true.

> *The full story is told in ' The Adventures of Sajo and her Beaver People', by Grey Owl.*

THE BEAVER PEOPLE

CHAPTER ONE

The Home of the Beaver People

RIGHT across the front of a small, deep pond, and blocking the bed of the stream that came out of it, was a thick, high wall of sticks and brush. It was all very tightly woven, and the chinks were filled with moss and the whole business well cemented with mud. Along the top of it a number of heavy stones had been placed to keep it solid. It was nearly one hundred feet long and more than four feet high, and the water flowed over the top of it through a narrow trough of sticks, so that the stream was wearing away at it in only this one spot, where it could be easily controlled. So well had it been made that it looked exactly as if a gang of men had been working at it—but it was animals, not men, that had built it.

This wall, which was really a dam, seemed as if it were holding the lake in place: which is really what it was doing, for without it there would have been no lake at all, only the stream running through.

The pond was bright with sunshine; very silent and peaceful it was, and so calm, that the few ducks dozing quietly upon its waters seemed almost to be floating on air, and the slim white poplar trees that stood upon its banks were reflected so plainly on its smooth surface, that it was hard to tell where the water stopped and the trees began. It was very beautiful, like a fairy-land, with its silver poplars and May flowers and blue water. And it was very still, for nothing moved there, and it seemed quite lifeless except for the sleeping ducks. Yet, had you watched patiently for a little while, being careful not to move or talk, or even whisper, you would have seen, before very long, a ripple on the water near the shore as a dark brown head, with round ears that showed very plainly, peered cautiously out from the rushes at the water's edge, and watched and listened and sniffed. The head was followed by a furry body, as its owner now came out in full sight and swam rapidly, but without a sound, to another place on the far shore, there to disappear among the reeds. The tall reeds swayed and shook for a minute as he worked there, and then he reappeared, this time holding before him a large bundle of grass, and swam over towards an enormous black mound of earth that we had been wondering about all this time, and dived, bundle and all, right in front of it. He had scarcely disappeared before another head, with another bundle, could be seen swimming from a different direction when—somebody moved, and with no warning at all, a huge flat tail came down on the water with a heavy smack, and with a mighty splash and a plunge the head and its bundle were gone. That great mound, taller than any of us, before which the swimmers had dived, was a beavers' house, and the dark brown, furry heads were those of the Beaver People themselves. And they had been very busy.

The lodge had been built up to more than six feet in height, and was a good ten feet across. It had lately been well plastered with wet mud, and heavy billets of wood had been laid on the slopes of it to hold everything firmly in place. It all looked very strong and safe-looking, like a fortress, and even a moose could have walked around on top of it without doing it a bit of harm. Up the side of it there was a wide pathway, on which the building materials were carried, and had you been more patient or careful awhile ago, or perhaps had the wind not played a trick on you and given you away to those keen noses, you might have seen old father beaver dig out a load of earth from the shore, go with it to the house, swimming slowly and carefully so as not to lose any, and then, standing upright like a man, walk to the top of the roof with the load in his arms and there dump it, pushing it into nooks and crannies with his hands, and shoving a good-sized stick in after it to keep it there.

And all this work had been done with a purpose. It was a very important time, this Month of Flowers, May, for inside that queer-looking home, hidden away from the eyes of all the world, were four tiny little kitten-beavers. Woolly little fellows they were, perfectly formed, with bright black eyes, big webbed hind feet, little hand-like fore-paws and tiny, flat, rubbery-looking tails. They had marvellous appetites, and their lungs must have been very good too, for they were the noisiest little creatures imaginable, and cried con-

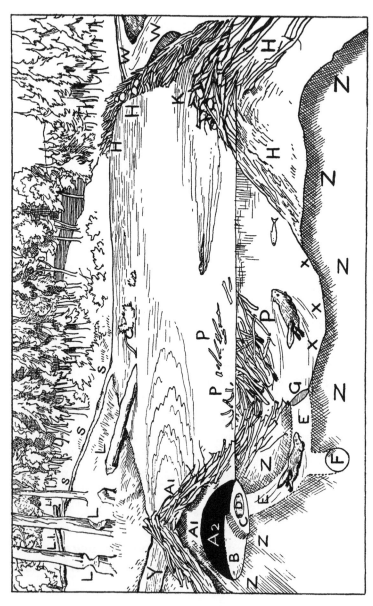

Beavers' Work

KEY TO DIAGRAM OF BEAVERS' WORK ON PAGE 80

A. 1, A. 1.	Beavers' house.
A. 2.	Interior of beavers' house. The living-room, or chamber.
B.	Sleeping platform.
C.	Lower level for drying off, draining into plunge-hole, at D.
D.	Plunge-hole.
E, E.	Tunnel leading out into deep water.
F.	Side, or emergency entrance, also used in discarding old bedding and used sticks.
G.	Main entrance.
H, H.	The dam.
K.	Spillway, for regulating overflow, and maintaining correct water level.
L, L, and L, I.	Trees felled, and partly felled by beavers.
P, P.	Feed-raft. Greatest portion under water, below the reach of ice.
S, S.	Beavers' runway, or hauling trail, used for removing required portions of tree, cut down by beavers, and marked L, I.
W, W.	Original stream resuming its course.
Y.	Stream running into pond, passing out at K.
X, X.	Bottom of pond has been dug out below the feed-raft and in front of the dam, so as to obtain a greater depth of water. The materials thus obtained are used in the construction of the dam and house.
Z, Z.	Former dry land, now under water on account of dam. Without the dam there would be no pond, only the stream.

REMARKS

(i) The house may be built close to the dam, but is often a considerable distance from it.

(ii) Note that the water level is exactly even with the plunge-hole.

(iii) Note that the swimming beavers have their front paws tucked up against their chests. The hind feet only are used in swimming, the front paws being used as hands, for working and picking up objects, or as feet for walking. Beavers do a considerable amount of walking on their hind feet, marching along slowly but very steadily; all loads consisting of earth, mud, or other loose materials, are carried in the arms, the beavers walking upright, like a man. The heavier sticks are drawn by means of the teeth, on all fours.

(iv) Beavers never use their tails for working in any way, except as a support in walking erect, or as a balancing-pole when clambering amongst fallen trees. In the water the tail is used as a rudder, sometimes as an oar, and for signalling by splashing on the water. This slapping sound is varied slightly, according to whether it is intended for an alarm signal, or as an indication of the owner's whereabouts. The kittens sometimes take a ride on their parents' tails.

tinuously in long, loud wails that were very much like the cries of small human babies: and like any other babies, they needed a great deal of attention—and you may be sure that they were getting a lot of it too.

The living-room, or chamber, inside the lodge, was large enough for a man to have curled up in it with ease, and was very clean and sweet smelling, with its floor of willow bark and bed of scented grasses. The entrance was through a short, slanting tunnel, one end of which, called the plunge-hole, was in the floor, and the other end came out below, near the bottom of the lake. The dam held the pond up to a level nearly even with the floor, keeping the plunge-hole always full, so that the tiny kittens, who were a little wobbly on their legs as yet, could drink there without falling into it; or if they did (which happened rather regularly), they could climb out again quite easily. The whole tunnel and the outer doorway were under water, so that no land animals could enter, or even see it, unless they were first-class divers, which most of them are not. But if the dam should break and let the saved-up water out, the beavers would be in grave danger, as not only could their enemies, such as wolves and foxes, find their way into the house, but the beavers would be unable to protect or hide themselves by diving suddenly out of sight, as you saw them do a little while ago.

If you look at the sketch you can see how it was all arranged, and will be able to realise how very important this dam was, and why the father spent so much of his time watching it and fixing any small leaks that appeared. He had, too, a pretty steady job keeping the trough, which you might call a regulator, clear of rubbish, so that the water could flow freely and not become too high, and so flood the house, but was always at exactly the right level. Between whiles, both he and the mother attended to their babies' every want, changing their bedding every so often, bringing in small sprays of tender leaves for them to eat, combing and brushing their wool (you could hardly call it fur), while they made queer, soft sounds of affection and talked to them in that strange beaver language that, at a little distance, sounds almost as though human people were speaking together in low voices. And the shrill wailing cries of the little ones, and their chattering, and their little squawks and squeals, could be heard even through the thick walls of the lodge, so noisy were they when they were hungry, or pleased or in some small trouble, which, one way and another, was pretty nearly all the time. And when either their father or their mother returned (they were never away together; one or the other was always on guard) from a trip to the so-important dam, or brought in new bedding of sweet-grass, he or she would give a low, crooning sound of greeting, to be immediately answered by a very bedlam of loud shouts of welcome from the youngsters, that went on long after it was at all necessary. They were never still unless they were asleep, and were continually scrambling around, and tussling together, and clambering over everything, and by the noise they made, seemed to be enjoying themselves immensely. And altogether they were pretty much like any other family, and were very snug and happy in their home.

The little ones were now old enough to try their hand at swimming in the plunge-hole, though at present this exercise consisted mostly in lying on top of the water, not always right side up, and going round and round in circles, screeching with excitement. And being so very light, and their fluffy coats containing so much air, they could not seem to sink deep enough for their webbed hind feet to get a grip on the water both at the same time, so they swam with first one foot and then the other, rolling from side to side and bobbing up and down, squirming and squealing and wriggling, while their parents passed anxiously around amongst them, giving them encouragement, or perhaps advice, in their deep, strong voices. From what I have seen of such goings on, it must have been rather a troublesome time for the old folks, this business of learning to swim, but the youngsters seemed to be having a good time, which, as you will agree, is, after all, something to be considered.

But they would soon become tired, and climbing out on to the drying-off place (a little lower than the rest of the floor, so the water would soak away and not run all over the beds), every little beaver carefully squeezed, rubbed and scrubbed the water from his coat on the front, sides, back, every place he could reach, sitting upright and working very industriously, puffing and blowing like most of us do after a swim. Then, when this was all over and everybody was dry, or thought he was (some of them would topple over once in a while and made rather a poor job of it), the call for lunch would go up in a loud chorus, and the new green leaflets and water plants that had been provided ahead of time (with the idea, no doubt, of putting a stop to the uproar as soon as possible), would be divided up, and pretty soon all the busy little jaws would be munching away, and the piercing cries died down to mumbles and little mutterings of contentment. And soon the little voices became quiet and the small black eyes closed, while they lay cuddled together on their sweet-smelling, grassy bed, with their tiny fore-paws, so much like hands, clutched tightly in each other's fur.

This would be their daily programme until, after perhaps three weeks, would come that glorious day when they would venture down the long, dim tunnel out into the brightness of the great unknown world that was all about them, but which they had never seen. And while they slept, the old ones stood watch and guard, turn about, and took turns to inspect the defences of their castle and the dam on which their very lives depended, and kept a weather eye out for enemies, and collected food and bedding for when the babies should awaken, and carried on at the hundred and one jobs that make father and mother beaver a very busy pair of people during the latter part of May, the Month of Flowers.

From *The Adventures of Sajo and her Beaver People.*

CHAPTER TWO

McGinty and McGinnis

AFTER open water on until early in June, the Spring hunt is in full swing on the frontier, and towards the end of that period the young beavers are born. The mother, who lives at this time in a separate lodge built and tended by the male or buck beaver, being generally larger than the rest of the family, is much sought after. She is easily caught close to the house, and drowns at the entrance, whilst the kittens within listen in terror to her frantic struggles to escape. Crying continuously in child-like wails, they wait in vain for the big kindly brown body that is supporting their feeble existence, till the thin little voices are stilled, and two pitifully small bundles of fur cease to move, and lie in the house to rot.

A neighbouring hunter once came to me and asked if I would come and remove a live beaver from a trap from which the drowning-stone had come loose. After several hours' travelling we arrived at the spot, when my companion refused to go to the trap, saying he could not bring himself to inflict any further torture on the suffering creature.

'Wait till you see,' he told me.

I went to the place he described, and this is what I saw.

'*The beaver, moaning with pain, was shaking the trap that was firmly clamped on one front foot.*'

The beaver, a large female, moaning with pain, was shaking the trap that was firmly clamped on one front foot, and with the other she held close to her breast, nursing it, a small kitten-beaver, who, poor little fellow, little knew how close he was to having his last meal.

I liberated her as gently as possible, and she made no effort to bite me.

With a sharp blow of my axe I severed the crushed and useless paw, when, parched with thirst, she immediately commenced to drink the blood which flowed from the wound as though it had been water. She then made slowly and painfully for the lake, only to return for the young one, who had become intensely interested in my footwear and was with difficulty prevailed on to enter the water. My companion approved of my action, although he had lost a valuable hide; he had seen the young one there, he said, and his heart had turned to water. This experience gave me some food for thought, and had its effect in hastening a decision I later arrived at, to give up the beaver hunt altogether.

Since that occurrence I have been the means of saving several pairs of small lives by following the carcase-strewn trails of the spring hunters, keeping the little fellows for about a year, after which period they get too reckless with the furniture to be any further entertained as guests.

Only those who have had the opportunity of studying living specimens over an extended period can obtain any idea of the almost human mentality of these likeable little creatures. Destructive they are, and their activities have much the same effect on the camp that two small animated sawmills running loose would have. They resemble somewhat an army tank, being built on much the same lines, and progressing in a similar manner, over or through anything that is in the way. After the first six months they can sink themselves through a six-inch log at a remarkable speed, biting lengthways with the grain of the wood for three or four inches, cutting the cross-section at each end and pulling out the chip.

They roam around the camp, and, with no evil intent but apparently from just sheer joy of living, take large slices out of table-legs, and chairs, and nice long splinters out of the walls, and their progress is marked by little piles and strings of chips. This is in the forepart of the evening. After 'lights out' the more serious work commences, such as the removal of deerskin rugs, the transferring of firewood from behind the stove into the middle of the floor, or the improvement of some waterproof footwear by the addition of a little open-work on the soles. They will gnaw a hole in a box of groceries to investigate, and are very fond of toilet soap, one brand in particular preferred, owing, no doubt, to the flavour incident to its school-girl complexion-giving qualities.

In Winter they will not leave the camp and I sink a small bath-tub in the floor for them, as they need water constantly. They make a practice of lying in the tub eating their sticks and birch-tops, later climbing into the bunk to dry themselves. To accomplish this, they sit upright and squeeze and scrub the entire body. The water never penetrates beyond the guard hairs into the fur, but I suppose half a pint is no exaggeration of the amount of water one of them will squeeze out of his coat.

Tiring of this performance, I once removed the bench by which they climbed into the bunk and prepared for a good night's rest at last. I had got so used to the continuous racket they created all night, between the drying-off periods, that, like the sailor who hired a man to throw pails of water against the walls of his house all night while on shore, I could not sleep so well without the familiar sounds, and during the night I awoke to an ominous silence. With a premonition of evil, I lit the lamp and on taking stock saw one of my much-prized Hudson Bay blankets hanging over the edge of the bunk, and cut into an assortment of fantastic patterns, the result of their efforts to climb into the bed. The regularity of the designs startled me, and I began to wonder if I had gone suddenly insane, as nothing short of human agency, it seemed, could have cut those loops and triangles so symmetrically. Closer examination showed that the effect had been produced by their gathering the blanket in bunches with their forepaws, and cutting out a few pieces from the pucker, with more or less pleasing results.

Apparently realising, by the tone of certain carelessly worded remarks which I allowed to escape me, that they had gone a little too far this time, the guilty parties had tactfully retired to their trench under the wall, awaiting developments. This excavation they had made themselves. In building the camp I had made an aperture in the bottom log, and constructed outside it, at great trouble, what was, I considered, a pretty good imitation of a beavers' house. The first night in they had inspected my work, found it unsuitable, and proceeded to block up the entrance with sacking. They then commenced operations under the bunk, cutting a hole in the floor for the purpose, and digging out the soil. This dirt they trundled up from the depths, pushing it ahead of them, walking with the hind feet only, the fore-paws and chin being used to hold the mass together. Whilst thus engaged they rather resembled automatic wheelbarrows. They brought up, on each journey, perhaps the full of a two-quart measure apiece of earth, which was painstakingly spread on the floor as it accumulated; as the tunnel was dug out for about six feet beyond the wall, there was quite an amount of dirt brought into the shack, and there were times when I, also, was quite busy with a shovel. They took my interference in good part, hopping and capering about my feet in their clumsy way, much as I imagine elephants would gambol. They eventually got pretty well organised, one sleeping and the other working in shifts of two or three hours each.

After about a week of this a large mound of earth was eventually patted down smooth and solid near the water supply, and operations apparently brought to a satisfactory conclusion; so I considered that we should all now take a good rest. But the beaver is not a restful animal. Doubtless they had been warned by those advertisements that remind us that 'those soft foods are ruining our teeth', for anything that offered resistance enough was bitten, the harder the better. Anything that gave good tooth-holds was hauled, and everything that could be pushed was pushed high, west, and sideways. Quantities of birch bark were carried into the bunk and shredded, this contribution to the sleeping accommodation supposedly entitling them to a share of the blankets. They apparently took notice that I put wood into the stove at intervals, and in a spirit, no doubt, of co-operation, at times they piled various articles against the stove. Once, when I had been out for a short time, I returned to find the camp full of smoke, and a pillow, a deer-skin rug, and a map of some value to me, piled around the stove, and all badly scorched. Eventually I was obliged to erect a wire screen for safety.

It is remarkable that, in spite of the orgy of destruction that went on for the first two weeks in camp, the door, an easy target, was not molested, and nothing was cut that would occasion an air leak into the camp. It is their nature to bank up against the intrusion of cold, and any loose materials that they could gather would be piled along the foot of the door, where there was a certain amount of draught. They barred the door so effectually on one occasion that I had to remove a window to enter the cabin.

Some mornings, at daylight, I would awaken to find one on each side of me sleeping, lying on their backs snoring like any human. At intervals during sleep they sharpen their teeth in readiness for the next onslaught. When working, if the teeth do not seem to be in good shape, they pause for half a minute or so and sharpen them, repeating this until they are suited. The skull is fitted with a longitudinal slot which allows for the necessary motion of the jaws, and the resultant grinding is much like the whetting of an axe. The sound of an axe or knife being filed struck them with terror, and they would drop everything and run to me for protection, evidently thinking the noise came from some large animal whetting its teeth.

These queer little people are also good house-keepers. Branches brought in for their feed are immediately seized on and piled to one side of the entrance to their abode. After feeding on pancakes or bread pudding, which they dearly love, the dish is pushed away into some far corner, along with the peeled sticks and other used portions of feed. Their beds, consisting of sacks, which they tear to shreds, mixed with shredded birch-bark and long, very fine shavings cut from the floor, after being used for a period, are brought out and scattered on the floor, apparently to dry, and taken in again after a couple of days. They spend long periods on their toilet. One of the toes of the webbed hind feet is jointed so as to bend in any direction, and is fitted with a kind of double claw; with this they comb their entire coat.

They seem capable of great affection, which they show by grasping my clothing with their strong forepaws, very hands in function, pushing their heads into some corner of my somewhat angular person, bleating and whimpering. At times they clamour for attention, and if taken notice of they shake their heads from side to side, rolling on their backs with squeals of joy.

In common with most animals when tamed, beavers will answer to a name. In Canada an Irishman is known as 'a Mick', and the Indian word for beaver, Ahmik, is identical in pronunciation. So I gave my pair Irish names, of which the two most notable were McGinty and McGinnis, names they got to know very well, and they were suitable in more ways than one, as they both had peppery tempers, and would fight anything or anybody, regardless of size, always excepting each other or myself.

My camp became known as 'The House of McGinnis', although McGinty, whimsical, mischievous as a flock of monkeys, being the female, was really the boss of the place.

From *The Men of the Last Frontier*.

CHAPTER THREE

Jelly Roll and Rawhide

JELLY ROLL

One unhappy day, McGinty and McGinnis wandered away and were never seen again. Grey Owl searched for them in vain, and at last he had to accept the fact of their loss; meantime he had found another kitten-beaver, and she soon became his close companion. Here is a picture of her when she had grown up.

HUNTING season passed and the woods became again deserted and we, this beaver and I, carried on our preparations for the Winter each at his own end of the lake. The outlet, near which my cabin was situated, passed through a muskeg, and the immediate neighbourhood was covered with spindling birch which I was rapidly using up for wood. Jelly had by far the best part of it so far as scenery was concerned, being picturesquely established at the mouth of a small stream that wandered down from the uplands through a well timbered gully. Here she lived in state. She fortified her burrow on the top with mud, sticks and moss, and inside it had a fine clean bed of shavings (taken from stolen boards), and had a little feed-raft she had collected with highly unskilled labour, and that had a very amateurish look about it. But she was socially inclined, and often came down and spent long hours in the camp. When it snowed she failed to show up, and I would visit her, and hearing my approach while still at some distance, she would come running to meet me with squeals and wiggles of welcome. We had great company together visiting back and forth this way, and I often sat and smoked and watched her working, and helped in any difficulties that arose. After the ice formed, her visits ceased altogether, and becoming lonesome for her I sometimes carried her to the cabin on my back in a box. She did not seem to mind these trips, and carried on a conversation with me and made long speeches on the way; I used to tell her she was talking behind my back. She made her own way home under the ice in some mysterious manner and always arrived safely, though I made a practice of following her progress along the shore with a flashlight, to make sure she did. This distance was over half a mile and I much admired the skill with which she negotiated it, though she cheated a little and ran her nose into muskrat burrows here and there to replenish her air supply. One night, however, after going home, she returned again unknown to me, and in the morning I found the door wide open and her lying fast asleep across the pillow. Nor did she ever go outside again, evidently having decided to spend the Winter with me; which she did. So I bought a small galvanised tank for her and sunk it in the floor, and dug out under one of the walls what I considered to be a pretty good imitation of a beavers' house interior.

Almost immediately on her entry, a certain independence of spirit began to manifest itself. The tank, after a lengthy inspection, was accepted by her as being all right, what there was of it; but the alleged beavers' house, on being weighed in the balance, was found to be wanting, and was resolutely and efficiently blocked up with some bagging and an old deer skin. She then dug out, at great labour, a long tunnel under one corner of the shack, bringing up the dirt in heaps which she pushed ahead of her and painstakingly spread over the floor. This I removed, upon which it was promptly renewed. On my further attempt to clean up, she worked feverishly until a section of the floor within a radius of about six feet was again covered. I removed this several different times with the same results, and at last was obliged to desist for fear that in her continued excavations she would undermine the camp. Eventually she constructed a smooth solid side walk of pounded earth clear from her tunnel to the water supply, and she had a well beaten playground tramped down all around her door. Having thus gained her point, and having established the fact that I was not going to have everything my own way, she let the matter drop, and we were apparently all set for the Winter. But these proceedings were merely preliminaries. She now embarked on a campaign of constructive activities that made necessary the alteration of almost the entire interior arrangements of the camp. Nights of earnest endeavours to empty the woodbox (to supply materials for scaffolds which would afford ready access to the table or windows) alternated with orgies of destruction, during which anything not made of steel or iron was subjected to a trial by ordeal out of which it always came off second best. The bottom of the door which, owing to the slight draught entering there, was a point that attracted much attention, was always kept well banked up with any materials that could be collected, and in more than one instance the blankets were taken from the bunk and utilised for this purpose. Reprimands induced only a temporary cessation of these depredations, and slaps and switchings produced little squeals accompanied by the violent twisting and shaking of the head, and other curious contortions by which these animals evince the spirit of fun by which they seem to be consumed during the first year of their life. On the few occasions I found it necessary to punish her, she would stand up on her hind feet, look me square in the face, and argue the point with me in her querulous treble of annoyance and outrage, slapping back at me right manfully on more than one occasion; yet she never on any account attempted to make use of her terrible teeth. Being in disgrace, she would climb on her box alongside me at the table, and rest her head on my knee, eyeing me and talking meanwhile in her uncanny language, as though to say, 'What are a few table legs and axe handles between men?' And she always got forgiven; for after all she was a High Beaver, Highest of All The Beavers, and could get away with things no common beaver could, things that no common beaver would ever even think of.

In spite of our difference in point of view on some subjects, we, this beast with the ways of a man and the voice of a child and I, grew very close during that Winter, for we were both of our kind, alone. More and more as time went on she timed her movements, such as rising and retiring and her meal-times, by mine. The camp, the fixtures, the bed, the tank, her little den and myself, these were her whole world.

Did I leave the camp on a two-day trip for supplies, my entry was the signal for a swift exit from her chamber, and a violent assault on my legs, calculated to upset me. And on my squatting down to ask her how things had been going in my absence, she would sit up and wag her head slowly back and forth and roll on her back and gambol clumsily around me. As soon as I unlashed the toboggan, every article and package was minutely examined until the one containing the never-failing apples was discovered. This was immediately torn open, and gathering all the apples she could in her teeth and arms, she would stagger away erect to the edge of her tank, where she would eat one and put the rest in the water. She entered the water but rarely, and after emerging from a bath she had one certain spot where she sat and squeezed all the moisture out of her fur with her fore-paws. She did not like to sit in the pool which collected under her at such times, so she took possession of a large square of birch bark for a bath-mat, intended to shed the water, which it sometimes did. It was not long before she discovered that the bed was a very good place for these exercises, as the blankets soaked up the moisture. After considerable inducement, and not without some heartburnings, she later compromised by shredding up the birch bark and spreading on it a layer of moss taken from the chinking in the walls. Her bed, which consisted of long, very fine shavings cut from the flooring and portions of bagging which she unravelled, was pushed out at intervals and spread on the floor to air, being later returned to the sleeping quarters. Both these procedures, induced by the requirements of an unnatural environment, were re-markable examples of adaptability on the part of an animal, especially the latter, as in the natural state the bedding is taken out and discarded entirely, fresh material being sought. The dish out of which she ate, on being emptied, she would shove into a corner, and was not satisfied until it was standing up against the wall. This trick seemed to be instinctive with all beavers, and can be attributed to their desire to pre-serve the interior of their habitation clear of any form of débris in the shape of peeled sticks, which are like-wise set aside in the angle of the wall until the owner is ready to remove them.

Any branches brought in for feed, if thrown down in an unaccustomed place, were drawn over and neatly piled near the water supply, nor would she suffer any sticks or loose materials to be scattered on the floor; these she always removed and relegated to a junk pile she kept under one of the windows. This I found applied to socks, moccasins, the wash board and the broom, etc., as well as to sticks. This broom was to her a kind of staff of office which she, as self-appointed janitor, was for ever carrying around with her on her tours of inspection, and it also served, when turned end for end, as a quick, if rather dry lunch, or something in the nature of a breakfast food. She would delicately snip the straws off it, one at a time, and holding them with one end in her mouth would push them slowly in, while the teeth, working at great speed, chopped it into tiny portions. A considerable dispute raged over this broom, but in the end I found it easier to buy new brooms and keep my mouth shut.

To fill her tank required daily five trips for water, and she got to know by the rattle of the pails when her water was to be changed. She would emerge from her seclusion and try to take an active part in the work, getting pretty generally in the way, and she insisted on pushing the door to between my trips, with a view to excluding the much dreaded current of cold air. This was highly inconvenient at times, but she seemed so mightily pleased with her attempts at co-operation that I made no attempt to interfere. Certain things she knew to be forbidden she took a delight in doing, and on my approach her eyes would seem to kindle with a spark of unholy glee and she would scamper off squealing with trepidation, and no doubt well pleased at having put something over on me. Her self-assertive tendencies now began to be very noticeable. She commenced to take charge of the camp. She, so to speak, held the floor, also anything above it that was within her reach, by now a matter of perhaps two feet and more. This, as can be readily seen, included most of the ordinary fixtures. Fortunately, at this late season she had ceased her cutting operations, and was contented with pulling down anything she could lay her hands on, or climb up and get, upon which the article in question was subjected to a critical inspection as to its possibilities for inclusion into the ramparts of objects that had been erected across her end of the camp, and behind which she passed from the entrance of her dwelling to the bathing pool. Certain objects such as the poker, a tin can, and a trap she disposed in special places, and if they were moved she would set them back in the positions she originally had for them, and would do this as often as they were removed. When working on some project she laboured with an almost fanatical zeal to the exclusion of all else, laying off at intervals to eat, and to comb her coat with the flexible double claw provided for that purpose.

Considering the camp no doubt as her own personal property, she examined closely all visitors that entered it, some of whom on her account had journeyed from afar. Some passed muster, after being looked over in the most arrogant fashion, and were not molested; if not approved of, she would rear up against the legs of others, and try to push them over. This performance sometimes created a mild sensation, and gained for her the title of The Boss. Some ladies thought she should be called The Lady of the Lake, others The Queen. Jelly the Tub I called her, but the royal title stuck and a Queen she was, and ruled her little kingdom with no gentle hand.

From *Pilgrims of the Wild*.

RAWHIDE

With the coming of Spring, Jelly Roll no longer slept indoors; but now a new arrival caused some excitement.

Just before the leaves came I set a trap for a marauding otter, on a stream some distance away. Jelly, on account of her optimistic outlook on life, would fall an easy victim. One morning on visiting the trap I found it gone, and projecting from under a submerged log saw the tail of a beaver. On pulling the chain I found resistance, and hauled out a living beaver, an adult. He had a piece of his scalp hanging loose, and, half-drowned and scared almost to death, he made little attempt to defend himself. I removed the trap and took him home with me, tied up in a sack. His foot was badly injured, and being one of the.all-important hind, or swimming feet, I decided to try and repair the damage before I liberated him. For the first twenty-four hours he hid himself in the Boss's late apartment, emerging only to drink, and he ate not at all. At the end of that time he came out into the centre of the camp with every appearance of fear, but I was able to pick him up and speaking kindly to him, offered him an apple which he took. I worked on him all night doing my best to inspire confidence, and succeeded to the extent that, crippled as he was, he commenced a tour of the camp, examining everything including the door, which he made no attempt to bite through. In the course of his explorations he discovered the bunk, climbed into it up Jelly's chute, found it to his liking, and from then on ate and slept there, occasionally leaving it for purposes of his own, such as to dispose of his peeled sticks or to take a bath. He slept between my pillow and the wall, and nearly every night he became lonesome and came around to sleep in the crook of my arm till daylight, when he went back behind the pillow.

Although the weather was still cold I dared light no fire in the camp, as the noise of the stove drove him frantic; tobacco smoke caused him to hide away for hours. The operation of dressing his foot single handed was an undertaking of no mean proportions. It was swollen to an immense size, and two of the bones projected through the skin. His teeth were badly shattered from his attempts to break the trap, and it would be weeks before they were again serviceable. The loose portion of his scalp had dried, and hung from his head like a piece of wrinkled hide, so I severed it and named him after it, calling him Rawhide, a name he still retains and knows.

For two weeks I worked hard to save the injured foot, and to a certain extent succeeded, although I believe the antiseptic effect of the leeches which clustered in the wound on his subsequent return to natural conditions, completed a task that taxed my ingenuity to the utmost. Whether on account of the attention he received, or because labouring under the impression that I had saved his life, or from very lonesomeness, I cannot say, but the poor creature took a liking to me, hobbling around the camp at my heels, and crying out loudly in the most mournful fashion when I went out. These sounds on one occasion attracted the attention of the Boss, who forthwith raced up into the camp to ascertain the cause. On seeing a strange beaver she nearly broke her neck trying to get out of the camp, running in her haste full tilt into the door, which I had closed. She then reconsidered the matter, and returned to give the newcomer the once over. She at once decided that here was somebody who, being disabled, would be perfectly easy to beat up, which kind and chivalrous thought she immediately proceeded to put into execution. After a considerable scramble which ended in my having to carry the would-be warrior bodily down to the lake, objecting loudly, quiet was restored. She apparently resented the presence of a stranger in the home, no matter whose home; she ruled here as queen and had no intention of sharing her throne with anybody, it seemed, and I had to fasten the door from then on to keep her out.

On my patient becoming convalescent I bid him good luck and turned him loose, not without some feelings of regret, as he had become very likeable and affectionate. The next day, on visiting the domicile of the so-militant queen, I saw a beaver and called it over. The animal answered and swam towards me, and my surprise can be well imagined, when I recognised the now well-known voice and lines of the cripple. He came to the canoe with every sign of recognition, followed me down the full length of the lake, and crept behind me into the camp. While there, he lay for a time on a deer-skin rug, and whimpered a little and nibbled gently at my hands, and presently slipped away to the lake again. And this practice he continued, sometimes climbing, with assistance, on to my knees and there conducting an assiduous and very damp toilet. He had nothing to gain by these manoeuvres, and could have left at any time for parts unknown had he been so minded. While I cannot go so far as to say that he was grateful, there is little doubt but that the treatment he had received while sick and confined to the cabin had had its effect on him, for he haunted me and the camp environs, unless driven away by the Boss, whose treatment of him was little

short of brutal. She was insanely jealous and drove
him away from the camp repeatedly, and would not
allow him to approach me if she were present. On
more than one occasion she chased him far down the
stream below the outlet, where I could hear him crying
out; but he always stuck to his guns and came back.
In spite of her hostility he followed her around and did
everything she did, hobbling on his injured foot, emit-
ting plaintive little sounds, and seeming almost pitifully
anxious to fit into the picture and be one of the boys.
He even succeeded, after several failures, in climbing
into the canoe, only to be thrown out by the Boss, on
which I interfered. He somehow gave the impression
that he was starving for companionship, and Jelly
refusing his advances he turned to me. He did all these
unaccustomed things in such a dumb and humble way,
yet with such an air of quiet resolution about him, that
I always took his part against the more flamboyant
and self-sufficient Jelly Roll. And by this very quiet
insistence, this inflexible yet calm determination, this
exercise of some unexpected latent power within him,
he overcame one by one the obstacles imposed on him
by his new environment and found his place at last,
and eventually took control and became no more a
suppliant but a leader.

The Boss had for me the friendship that exists
between equals; we were rough and tumble playfellows, old-timers together who could take liberties
with one another and get away with it. But the

'*He even succeeded, after several failures, in climbing into the canoe,
only to be thrown out by the Boss.*'

stranger, for all his harsh sounding and rather unsuitable name of Rawhide, seemed to want only a little
kindness to make him happy, and was as gentle as the
touch of the night wind on the leaves; yet I once saw
him, driven to passion by too much persecution, shake
the Boss like she had been a paper bag.

And I think she owes it to him that she lives to-day.

A rogue beaver, old and watchful and wise, his
colony no doubt destroyed by hunters, now gone bad
and ranging far and wide, descended on these two
while I was away and tried to take possession. On my
return I found Jelly laid out on the landing before the
camp. A thin trail of blood led to the door but she
must have been too weak to enter, and had dragged
herself back to the water's edge to wait. Her throat
was torn open, some of the parts protruding; her
bottom lip was nearly severed, both arms were punc-
tured and swollen and nearly useless, and her tail had
been cut completely through at the root for over an
inch of its width and there were besides a number of
ugly gashes on the head and body. There was nothing
I could do save to disinfect the wounds. Meanwhile
she lay inert, her eyes closed, moaning faintly, while
her blood oozed away into the mud of the landing she
had so stoutly maintained as her own; and in her
extremity she had come to me, her friend, who could
only sit helplessly by, resolving to let her quietly die
beside her pond, where she had once been a small
lonesome waif, before she was a queen.

I sat beside her all night, and at intervals fed her with milk from a glass syringe. Towards morning she seemed to draw on some hidden resources of vitality and bestirred herself, and slowly, painfully, crawled up into the cabin; for I did not dare to pick her up for fear of opening up her now clotted wounds afresh. She stayed with me all that day, leaving again at night, in bad shape but with the best part of two cans of milk inside her, and apparently on the mend. Only the marvellous recuperative powers possessed by wild animals and man in a state of nature brought her round. I did not see her again for a week, but often passed the time of day with her through the walls of her abode, and heard her answer me. By the signs I discovered around the lake and from what I saw of him another time, the visitor must have been of enormous size, and there is no doubt that had she been alone she would have been killed. Rawhide also bore marks of the encounter, but to a less degree, and I am sure by what I have since seen of his other abilities, that his assistance must have turned the tide of battle.

From then on the two of them lived in perfect harmony, and have done ever since.

From *Pilgrims of the Wild*.

THE KEEPERS OF THE LODGE

Grey Owl's success in befriending the beavers attracted the notice of the Canadian Government, and it was decided to establish him in the Prince Albert National Park, Saskatchewan. So off he went with Jelly Roll and Rawhide to their new home, Beaver Lodge, beside a lake. The beavers soon turned part of the log-cabin into half of their own home with the other half outside by the lake.

By this time Jelly Roll and Rawhide had become mates, and as time went by the cabin became the headquarters of several generations of their offspring.

Despite her affection and the disarming innocence of her softer moments, Jelly Roll is the most self-willed creature in all the world. She knows what is forbidden, and constantly attempts to outwit me; but on being caught red-handed, as she nearly always is (she is the most guileless, transparent old bungler imaginable when it comes to artifice), she flops down and flounders around in an apparent agony of fear, though she must know that she had nothing to fear but my disapproval and reproach, to which she is very sensitive indeed. On being comforted (a little later, of course), she will jump up at once and start to frolic; yet the lesson is not forgotten—not that day, anyway. A scolding from me puts her in the greatest misery, but a peremptory word or two, or an overt act, from another, causes instant and sometimes very active hostility. She has a strong instinct for protection towards her young, as has her partner. This is a trait possessed by most animals but, like some dogs, she goes further and, without training of any kind, stands with threatening attitude and voice between a stranger and myself, should I happen to be lying down. However, if I am standing up, I can darned well take care of myself. She herself has no fear whatsoever of strangers, and will face any crowd, and go among them, inspecting them and taking charge with the most unshakeable aplomb.

She has often stolen papers of some value to me, and gets all the envelopes from my correspondence, which is considerable. She has a preference for periodicals, as the advertising pages are on stiffer paper than is the reading matter, and they can be induced to make a more deliciously exciting noise, and when she gets hold of one of these she is beside herself with happiness, shaking her head back and forth as she walks out of the door with it, her whole person emanating triumphant satisfaction. Once, at the request of an onlooker who thought that her patriotism should be tested, I placed before her three separate magazines, Canadian, English, and American. After giving each one a searching examination, she chose the Canadian periodical and walked out with it. The visitor was rather taken aback, and still believes that I made some secret sign to her that she acted on. Pure accident, naturally, but the effect was quite good. Sometimes the sober Rawhide joined in these escapades, a few of which were positively uncanny, had they not been so utterly ridiculous.

Beavers like to have dry cedar on which to exercise their teeth, it being nice and crunchy. As there were no cedars in that particular area, I took a bundle of shingles that had been left over from the roofing of my new cabin, and left them down on the shore for the beavers' use. Next morning I found that the fastenings had been cut off and neatly laid to one side, and the whole of the shingles removed. I wondered what was the purpose of this wholesale delivery, until, the next afternoon, a man came to see me who wanted very much to see the beavers at work. It was a few minutes' walk to the beavers' house, and as we drew near to it I noticed that it had a strange appearance, and arriving there we, this man and I, stood perfectly still and stared, and stared, and *stared—one side of the beavers' house was partly roofed with shingles!*

At length my visitor asked in a hushed voice, 'Do you see what I see?' I replied that I did. 'Exactly!' he agreed. 'We're both crazy. Let's get out of here.' We retired, I remember, in awe-struck silence, went to the cabin and drank quantities of very strong tea. I asked him if he didn't care to wait and see the beavers themselves, and he shook his head. 'No,' he answered, 'I don't believe I do. I'm not long out of the hospital and just couldn't stand it, not to-day. Some other time—' and went out of there muttering to himself. The explanation is, of course, quite simple. Beavers will seize on any easily handled material they find, and make use of it for building purposes (this includes firewood, paddles, dish-pans, clothing, etc.), and seized on the shingles at once, and being unable to push the shingles, owing to their oblong shape, into the mesh of the structure, had just left them lying there on the sides of the house.

But the star performance was one of Jelly's very own. One afternoon, shortly after the affair of the shingles, I heard a woman's scream, long and piercing, from the direction of the beavers' dam. Beside the dam ran the trail that led to my cabin. Now Jelly is a real watch-dog when I am not around, and at that time, in her younger days, would lie in ambush, waiting for people so she could chase them (a practice since abandoned), and thinking she had caught somebody in her ambuscade and was scaring them to death, I hustled down to the dam to see about it. I found there a woman, evidently badly frightened, who exclaimed: 'Do you know what I have just seen?—a beaver going by with a paint brush!' 'A who going by with a what?' I demanded. 'A *beaver* going by with a *paint brush*!' she affirmed. 'Oh, I know you won't believe me, but that's what I saw.' Accustomed though I was to the hare-brained exploits of these versatile playmates of mine, this rather floored me, so I simply said, 'Oh!' and led the woman to the cabin. I left her there and went to the stump on which the man who had been painting the new roof had left his paint brush. Sure enough, it was gone, removed by busy fingers whose owner was always on the watch for something new. So I told this to the lady, and the matter was explained. But it never was explained to me why, later in the evening, I should find lying at the foot of the stump, with the fresh imprint of four very sharp incisor teeth upon it, the missing paint brush. Why was it returned? Your guess is as good as mine.

And reader, believe it or not, all during the latter part of this last paragraph, a beaver of the third, or inexperienced generation, finding that his efforts to open the door have been persistently disregarded, has been trying to get in through the window. It will, I think, be cheaper, in the long run, to open the door. I have opened the door, and there are three beavers; I'll be seeing you later, reader.

To resume. To-day there were a large number of visitors here. The moose, a great bull with his antlers half developed, but for all that wide and formidable-looking enough, obligingly stalked down within a distance of a few yards and had a look at the crowd. They also, with mingled feelings, had a look at him. But Jelly Roll, after all the complimentary things I have written about her, let me down rather badly. Having demolished a chocolate bar offered her by a lady, she turned her back on the entire assemblage, took a branch I proffered, smelled it, threw it to one side, launched herself into the lake, and was no more seen. This behaviour is not usual with her. In fact, at times she is rather difficult to get away from, and is one of those ladies who do *not* take 'No' for an answer. She is very self-assertive, and has no intention of being overlooked when there is any company around or anything especially good to eat to be had. At these times she is very much to the fore, assuming a bustling and extremely proprietary manner, and whether excited by the presence of strangers or on account of the reward she has come to know that she will get, or from sheer devilment, I cannot pretend to say, but she will very often stage a little act. She first inspects one by one the visitors who, by the way, are seated well out of the way in the bunk—she thoroughly enjoys a taste of good shoe leather—and if pleased, which she generally is, she commences her show. This consists in trundling back and forth the bag of papers, the removal perhaps of the contents of the bag, with resultant rumpus and mess, the replacing of sticks removed by me from the beavers' house for that purpose, and various other absolutely unnecessary evolutions. And all this with such an air of earnestness and in such breathless excitement, and with such manifest interest in the audience and such running to and fro to them between the scenes, that those present could be excused for supposing it to be all for their especial benefit. We have, of course, a slight suspicion that the anticipated reward may have some bearing on this excessive display. But a good time is had by everyone present, and that is all that really matters. Speaking to her conversationally attracts her instant, if casual attention, and often elicits a response. She has come to understand the meaning of a good deal of what I say to her; but this faculty is not confined by any means to her alone. The beaver is an animal that holds communication by means of the voice, using a great variety of inflections, very human in character, and the expression and tone indicate quite clearly to human ears what emotions they are undergoing; and this resemblance makes it fairly easy for them to understand a few simple words and expressions. I have made no attempt to train them in this, or in anything else; everything they do is done of their own free will, and it has all been very free and easy and casual. I do not expect them to knuckle down to me, and I would think very little of them if they did; nor do I let them dominate me. We are all free together, do as we like, and get along exceedingly well together. Rawhide I know, for one, would not tolerate for a moment any attempt to curtail his freedom or to curb his independent spirit. He is rather a solemn individual, and he ignores nearly everything that is not directly connected with his work and family. Yet even he has his times to play, and carries always about him an undefinable air of 'howdy folks and hope everything's all right and it's a great world'. The obstinacy of a beaver when opposed by any difficulty also applies if you try to get him to do anything against his will, but personal affection has a great influence on their actions, and given sufficient encouragement and a free hand they will learn, of themselves, to do a number of very remarkable things quite foreign to their ordinary habits. Rawhide, for instance, has learned to kick open the door when walking erect with a load in his arms. He built his house inside mine, and will climb into a canoe and enjoy a ride, as does his life partner. Jelly Roll is able to open the camp door with ease from either side, pushing it open widely to come in, and making use of a handle I have affixed to the bottom of the door to get out again. And as the door swings shut of itself, she has succeeded in creating the impression that she always closes the door behind her, which is all to the good. Though he rarely answers me as Jelly does, Rawhide listens closely, with apparent understanding, when I talk to him, and dearly loves to be noticed, often rushing up to me when I meet him by chance on a runway, and clasping my fingers very firmly in his little hands. But his old, wild instincts are very strong in him, nor do I try to break them; and he has not bothered to learn very many of Jelly's tricks, being, it would seem, quite above such monkey work. But he will come at my call, when disposed to do so, and can be summoned from his house upon occasion, he selecting the occasion.

In the more serious matters, however, Rawhide plays a more notable part, being direct in all his actions, and rather forceful in his quiet way, and in family matters is something of a martinet. For instance, he took a strong objection to Jelly Roll sleeping in my bed, at a time when they lived together with me in the cabin. She had been always used to sharing my bed and no doubt expected to keep it up all her life. But when he would awaken and find her absent from his couch, he would emit loud wailing noises, and come over and drive her away into their cubby-hole. To see him pushing her ahead of him, she expostulating in a shrill treble of outraged sensibilities, was about as ludicrous an exhibition as I have ever seen, and when with childish squeals she would break away and rush to me for protection from this unwelcome discipline, her wonted dignity all gone, she would stick her head in under my arm and lie there like the big tub she is, imagining herself safe, but leaving her broad rear end exposed to his buffeting. And this ostrich-like expedient availed her very little, for Rawhide is about the most determined creature I ever knew, and always gained his point. And from then on, not wishing to be the cause of further family discord, I discontinued my habit of sleeping on the floor.

But don't get the impression that Jelly only plays and never works. She does both with equal enthusiasm. Jelly, when on labour bent, fairly exudes determination. She will arrive at a runway under a great head of steam, and on striking shore there is no perceptible pause for changing gears; she just keeps on, out, and up, changing from swimming to walking without losing way. Her progress on land is not so much a walk as it is the resolute and purposeful forward march of a militant crusader, bent on the achievement of some important enterprise. Her mind made up,

'*Learned to kick open the door when walking erect with a load in his arms.*'

without further ado she proceeds immediately to the point of attack, and by an obstinate and vigorous onslaught will complete in a remarkably short space of time, an undertaking out of all proportion to her size. She accepts my occasional co-operation right cheerfully, but being, as she is, an opportunist of the first water, instead of making a fair division of labour she sees her chance to get that much more work done, and attempts to haul sticks of timber or move loads that are more than enough for the two of us, attacking the project with an impetuous violence that I am supposed, apparently, to emulate. Her independence of spirit is superb, and she blandly disregards my attempts to set right any small mistakes I think she has made (a practice I have long ago desisted from). She is pretty shrewd and belongs to that rare type of worker who finds the day all too short for his purpose.

Though not very demonstrative, Rawhide has his softer moments too, and in a way that seems so very humble, as though he knew that Jelly had some method of expression that he can never have but does the best he can. But this is only when everything is properly squared away and he has time on his hands. For he is methodical in this as in all his ways. And if he does permit himself a little space for play, it is not for long, and becoming suddenly serious, as though he felt that he had committed himself in a moment of weakness, he walks or swims very soberly away. He has a fine regard for the niceties too, and never interferes in conversation or speaks out of his turn, as Jelly often does. A visitor once said that Rawhide reminded him of some old man who had worked too hard when very young, and never had his childhood.

This methodical beast is something of an unsung hero; not that he does actually a great deal more than Jelly, but he is less spectacular and attracts less notice. Yet most of the undertakings that have been completed here bear the stamp of his peculiar methods and devising. His studious attention to what he deems to be his duty, his quiet competence, and his unruffled and unconquerable poise, are on a different plane to Jelly's violently aggressive, but none the less effective programme. And as he sits sometimes so motionless, regarding me so steadily with his cool and watchful eye, I often wonder what he thinks of me.

Jelly Roll, jovial, wayward and full of whims.
Rawhide, calm, silent and inscrutable.
These two; King and Queen of All the Beaver People,
These are the Keepers of the Lodge.

From *Tales of an Empty Cabin.*

GLOSSARY

Abitibi. This river flows from a lake of the same name, northwards into Hudson Bay from eastern Ontario.

Ajawaan. The lake where Grey Owl had his cabin. It is situated in the Prince Albert National Park, about one hundred miles north of the town of Prince Albert in central Saskatchewan.

babiche. See below, 'Snowshoe'.

bannock. A form of bread made with flour, water and baking-powder, baked in the ashes or in a fry-pan. Eaten fresh, and dipped in hot lard or pork-grease.

bridle. See below, 'Snowshoe'.

brigade. Consists of four canoes or more, but loosely applied to parties of any size.

buckskin. A soft leather made of deer or other skin. Caribou or reindeer skin does not stretch when wet. The buckskin jacket or hunting shirt keeps out the wind, remains soft, will not catch on thorns, and wears for ever. The fringes are not purely orna-mental, as in rain the water drips off them and the shirt dries better.

caribou. North-American reindeer.

Cree. A tribe of North-American Indians of Algonquin stock, like the Ojibways. The Crees occupied the region round Lake Winnipeg and the Saskatchewan River. Their chief enemies were the Blackfoot tribe.

Fall. Autumn; the season when the leaves fall. The term is chiefly used now in North America, but it is also an old English word.

Fire Rangers. These men are employed by the Canadian Govern-ment to patrol the vast forest areas to fight the menace of fire. Incalculable damage has been done, and is still done, by forest fires, which may devastate thousands of square miles of country. For a fuller description of the fire-service, the chapter entitled 'The Altar of Mammon' in *The Men of the Last Frontier* should be read. Aeroplanes are now used for patrol work, as well as an elaborate system of outlook towers, etc.

Hudson's Bay Company, generally known as 'The Company'. The history of Canada is bound up with that of the H.B.C. The Company was founded in 1670 by Prince Rupert to promote the fur trade round the shores of Hudson Bay, in an area vaguely defined as Prince Rupert's Land. Gradually the Company extended its interests and its traders pushed westwards to the Rockies, and much early exploration was due to them. The trading posts were important links in the spread of the white man's influence. The story of the H.B.C. is a romance in itself.

Hudson Bay blanket. Originally made for the servants of 'The Company', this blanket soon became an article of trade on account of its excellent qualities; to say 'Hudson Bay blanket' is equivalent to saying 'Rolls-Royce car'.

husky. The Eskimo sledge-dog; a semi-wild animal of mixed breed, but of great endurance.

Indian. Grey Owl rightly objected to the term 'Red Indian'. He said it was 'too suggestive of the dime novel and blood-and-thunder literature'. The correct term is 'North-American Indian'. Grey Owl had a high opinion of the knowledge of Indian life and customs shown in Longfellow's *Hiawatha*, and he recognised that Fenimore Cooper 'must have done some travelling with Indians'. The North-American Indians, before the white man came, lived in tribes; each tribe had a hunting area large enough to allow for wandering in search of game. They were nomadic and lived in wigwams, or teepees, which could be moved easily. This life made the men experts in woodcraft and backwoodsmanship, and they have never had their equals. With the coming of the white man, the numbers of Indians decreased through the introduction of new diseases, the sale of spirits, etc. To-day there are probably not more than 100,000 pure-bred Indians in the whole of North America. Some of the deterioration has been arrested by the formation of Indian Reservations, areas where the Indians can live their own lives and maintain their native customs. It is interesting to note that Indian blood—and there has been much intermarrying—is not regarded with the same distaste as black (slave) blood; indeed, many notable men in the United States and in Canada have Indian blood in their veins. Grey Owl claimed to be a half-breed, and took pride in his ancestry.

Indian Summer. A period of fine, mild weather during late autumn.

larrigan. An oil-tanned moccasin of heavy leather, sometimes having a hard sole.

Mississauga. A river running from the north into the North Channel of Lake Huron. Its mouth is about seventy miles east of Sault Sainte-Marie.

moccasins. Soft shoes made of moose-hide or inferior skin. There is no hard sole, and consequently they are ideal for woods travel, as the wearer can feel the ground under his feet and so avoid making alarming noises, such as treading on sticks, etc.

moose. The elk of North America and some parts of Northern Europe and Asia. Distinguished by its overhanging upper lip, and, in the male, by the wide-spread palmated antlers.

muskeg. Swampy ground.

Ojibway. An Indian tribe of Algonquin stock, and sometimes known by that name. They formerly hunted over lands on the north of Lakes Huron and Superior. Grey Owl was adopted by the Ojibways, who gave him his name Wa-Sha-Quon-Asin, 'he who walks by night'. He wrote: 'Half-breed trapper I am, and far more closely identified with the Ojibway Indians than any other people. I want the Ojibways to get their share of any credit that may accrue. I am their man. They taught me much.'

pan. The fan-shaped spread of the moose-antler.

peltry. Fur.

portage. A part of the trail where it is impossible to go by water; all gear must be carried overland to the next navigable stretch. Portages are divided into sections called 'stages', about six or eight minutes apart, that being the length of time experience shows a man can carry a big load without fatigue. He recuperates on the way back for the next load. This is an Indian system, and it has proved better to work in this fashion than by taking smaller loads right through.

Prince Albert. A town of some 12,000 inhabitants on the Saskatchewan River. To the north of it lies the Prince Albert National Park, where Grey Owl had his beaver lodge. There are a number of these National Parks in Canada; each is of considerable size, and remains a natural preservation of forest and lake; the public can use them for holidays, but not for hunting.

reservation, or reserve. *See above,* 'Indian'.

runway. A slope made for greater ease down to the shores of a lake, etc.

Saskatchewan. The central province of the prairie region of Canada.

shingle. A wooden roof-tile.

snowshoe. The Canadian snowshoe is so designed that its broad surface prevents the foot sinking into the snow. It is 3 to 5 ft. long, and 1 to 2 ft. wide. The largest are used by the man who goes ahead to break the trail. The snowshoe is roughly pear-shaped. The frame is made of tough wood, and a network of rawhide thongs (*babiche*) is interlaced between, rather like a tennis racket. There are two loops (*bridles*) into which the toes fit, while the heels are left free. The snowshoe lifts in front only and so crunches down the snow.

squaw. Indian woman.

teepee. Conical-shaped tent of skins or birch bark supported by poles.

Temagami. A lake in the Temagami Forest Reserve of Ontario; the Ottawa River is near.

tumpline. Two 10-ft. leather thongs attached to a broad band, which goes over the forehead; the thongs are fastened round the load, and the weight is thus partly taken by the head-band; especially useful in going uphill.

voyageur. A man employed by traders to carry goods from place to place. Used generally of Canadian canoe-men. A reminder of the days when Canada was French.

whiskey-jack. Common grey jay of Canada; also known as the camp-bird.

wigwam. General term for any Indian lodge, cabin or shelter.

www.ingramcontent.com/pod-product-compliance
Ingram Content Group UK Ltd.
Pitfield, Milton Keynes, MK11 3LW, UK
UKHW042147280225
455719UK00001B/151